Chasing Likes

The Unflattering Reality of Being an Influencer

CARLEE KRTOLICA

Chasing Likes: *The Unflattering Reality of Being an Influencer*

ISBN: 979-8-793-47642-3 (paperback)

First Edition

DEDICATION

To my girls, L and M. I hope that you always remain your authentic selves and never seek the approval of strangers.

Stay true to who you are. Be kind to others.
Don't feed Hattie from the table.

xoxo

Sierra,

Thank you for all the support — I hope you enjoy this book!

xoxo,

Callee

CONTENTS

ACKNOWLEDGMENTS

I have to take a moment here to acknowledge my husband, Vanja. The "Jack" to my "Jill of All Trades". He's my "Instagram husband", snapping most of my photos, editing them for light and proofreading some of my captions to ensure I don't come off as "old man yells at cloud". He's also my web designer, DIY reno muscle and the chef in our house (so I don't starve).

Thank you for your unending support, for helping me navigate the influencer space and for encouraging me to pursue writing this book...and then subsequently formatting it and designing the cover! I couldn't have done this without you, and I wouldn't want to do life with anyone else.

Thank you to my parents and all of the friends who read the early chapters of this book and told me that I really "had something" and encouraged me to keep writing. To everyone who read, re-read, and provided unfiltered notes, for the late-night conversations on these topics and the support throughout this process, thank you.

To those of you in the influencer industry who helped me navigate sharing what it is that we do for a living, I am very grateful.

INTRODUCTION

Hey there!

My name is Carlee and I've been a blogger and social media influencer since 2015. I'm just a regular girl who lives a regular but slightly extra-ordinary life and shares a very small part of that online. I have a modest following on social media and a successful career as an influencer and content creator. I figured since you're going to be reading this book that is filled with my personal experiences and anecdotes that it might be nice for you to get to know me a little first.

My Own Influencer (Success) Story

Everyone's story about how or why they got into the influencer industry is different. I personally fell into the influencer space without really realizing that's what was happening. I started a blog in 2015 and thought social media would play an important role in promoting my blog posts. What I didn't realize is that there was an entire industry that was going to be built around advertising products in exchange for money, all based on how many people were following me.

I am someone who naturally shares what they love with both friends and complete strangers, so when I was at a career crossroads, my husband proposed that I start a blog. When he made the suggestion, I honestly thought that blogs were something that students studying abroad wrote so that their aunts and grandmas could keep up with their adventures – I had no idea it was something that could be done as a real career.

I've always had the gift of the gab and no trouble offering unsolicited advice, to anyone who would listen. Whether it be about products I love and believed they should buy, travel suggestions for their next trip, lists of gift ideas for their loved ones, my favorite wines and/or design advice based on any of the renovation projects going on in our home.

My husband's suggestion: Why not get this information out to a wider audience? And so, it began.

Blogger First, Influencer Second

I thought that if I could get enough blog readers through publishing really informative content that I could make money through advertising revenue and affiliate links.

But then along came Instagram…

I initially started my Instagram as a miniature version of my blog, really just to promote my newest posts for free in an attempt to grow my readership. I didn't see the industry of being an influencer as something I would or even could do. My initials aren't "K.K." nor have I ever appeared on reality TV, so it wasn't on my radar as an option, let alone my accidental career path.

I gained most of my followers on Instagram before the days of the ever-changing algorithm. Instagram was still a simple photo-sharing app without stories or video content. Vine and SnapChat were still a thing but TikTok didn't exist yet. Just writing this makes me feel like I'm talking about a bygone era, but in some respects, I am. Social media has changed so rapidly just in the time that I've been using it that the pace of change is worth mentioning.

Building an audience isn't easy but it's also amazing. It's an incredible feeling to connect with others and inspire them, help them feel seen or offer advice when they need it. It's also a ton of fun having a group of modern-day pen pals who seek your advice and recommendations because they trust what you have to say.

However, with great influence comes great responsibility.

Why I Wrote This Book

There are so many questions, curiosities, and misconceptions about being an influencer. People are either fascinated by the industry and ask an overwhelming number of questions, or they are completely disgusted by the very thought of what I do for a living. "Oh, you're one of those" is something I heard from a customs agent, of all people, which is all the more reason to share what this industry and career are really like.

I wanted to share some of my experiences as an influencer and peel back the curtain on what it really takes to do this job. What influencers do is often misunderstood. Although it looks really glamourous from the outside, it isn't all gift boxes arriving at the door or invites to fancy parties.

There are a lot of skills required and even more hustle to make this into a legitimate career and I want to provide an honest perspective and give credit where credit is due.

I've also had a bit of an existential crisis as of late about what I do for a living and much of that is shared throughout this book. Don't get me wrong: I love what I do, but sometimes it feels like being an influencer is like working in the "wild west" since it's such an unregulated industry. It's not a surprise that the general public has begun to distrust influencers and there are a number of valid reasons as to why.

4

I often don't feel like I fit the typical influencer mould and thus don't want to be lumped in with that crowd.

I wanted to share this information with the world because there are those of us who have a real passion for doing this and they deserve to be acknowledged. Like with any other job or career, some do it with a purpose and desire to make an impact, and on the flip side there are others who are only in it for the money and in turn, damage the industry as a whole.

I personally love to be able to create meaningful content and get paid to share what I would naturally share with complete strangers. I've been fortunate to connect with some amazing people, partner with some incredible brands and make some amazing friends through working in this industry, and for that I am very thankful.

xoxo
Carlee

A Few Disclaimers

I'm not here to #humblebrag about the success I've had as an influencer. I'm sharing my own experiences for your information and (probably) entertainment. It's important to remember that these experiences are entirely my own.

84% of influencers identify as women and 100% of my experiences with other influencers have been with women. Most of the influencers that I know and follow are women, so throughout this book you will notice the pronoun "she" used more frequently than any other.

Although I am sharing several personal experiences in this book, I don't name names or share handles to protect the innocent.

Infer what you choose.

CHAPTER 1

ALMOST FAMOUS

Most influencers have built their miniature empires from nothing. They started a blog or an Instagram account and through sharing their daily outfits, renovation projects, recipes, makeup tips or anything and everything else in their lives they attracted an audience. Sooner or later, others started to take notice of what they were doing, and their follower count grew from friends and family to a legitimate group of devotees.

Some influencers started their accounts because they have a passion for something specific like fashion or beauty. Others love comparing products and sharing their findings as a service. Some are avid world travelers and love to share their experiences and advice. Others wanted a maternity leave hobby and thought that being semi-famous on Instagram would be a great way to get free stuff for their kids (because baby gear ain't cheap!). Some influencers do this because they don't want to work a traditional 9 to 5 or because they think it's easy money. Many do it purely for the fame and notoriety because for them, nothing beats the attention.

Not Everyone Starts from Nothing

For a few years it was the natural progression for former contestants appearing on any television show in *ABC's Bachelor* franchise to start marketing products to their newly grown Instagram audience (looking at you Fab Fit Fun Box and hair vitamin gummy bears!). Reality television contestants have been able to turn their five minutes of fame into a viable business where they are paid to host giveaways and sell products to an audience devoted to them simply because they were on a few episodes of a television show.

Most influencers, however, have built their audiences through hard work, determination, great content, and keen business acumen. We aren't *Bachelor* alums or reality stars. We don't have parents who were celebrity attorneys. Our careers weren't launched with sex tapes. We're just regular people living regular lives and sharing some of that life online.

Oh, For Fame

For the number of influencers out there that have grown an audience and gained some low-key fame for providing useful content or impacting the lives of others in a positive way, there are as many or more who have grown a following by posting bikini selfies with pointless captions. Their meaningless content only adds to the continuous watering-down of society. But hey, what do most kids now want to be when they grow up? Instagram famous, apparently.

Some influencers think that they're *actual* celebrities and act that way around other influencers, especially. They hold themselves in such high regard that they believe they should be fawned over by their peers and hope that onlookers will run up to take photos with them, if only to further demonstrate their celebrity status. They treat wait staff and retail workers at establishments they're collaborating with like peasants who should be worshipping them because they're "somebody".

I remember meeting a fellow-influencer in person at an event that I had been DM'ing with on and off for months and she behaved like we had never spoken before. I told her how nice it was to finally meet in-person and she replied with "I'm very recognizable" and then walked away. What does that even mean? Like, I'm *actually* asking.

Oversharing & Wannabe Reality Stars

You don't need to be on the *E! Network* to pretend that you're a *Real Housewife* of wherever you live. Social media has you covered; no television contract required. There are those among us who are natural over-sharers, divulging every personal detail imaginable to their social media as if it were mandatory. Couple that with an influencer career and you've got an amateur reality star, and for good reason. ***Drama sells.*** Even if their audience despises them and thinks they are a terrible human being, that audience can't pull their eyes away and that influencer's engagement will soar because of it.

Engagement numbers are like television ratings. It's a competitive game and once you're on the bike you can't stop peddling (pun intended), or you'll get left behind. But at what point did you go from relatable online personality to creating your own version of *EDtv*?[1]

What's a little startling about this is when you see influencers start to lose themselves in the attention that they're getting (or seeking; I can't decide). They start doing and saying more personal, outrageous, or self-deprecating things to continue the cycle without realizing the damage they could be doing to themselves (or society for that matter).

---

[1] EDtv is a 1999 film directed by Ron Howard, starring Matthew McConaughey

"I don't really think that, but you know, it's for the 'gram" is something I have heard countless women say when they've created posts and videos that seek to belittle their own intelligence or that of their friends, partner and family.

So you're cool with pretending you're stupid because it's trending, or for better engagement or relatability? Girl, we are very different people. Women have spent centuries trying to get society to take them seriously and view them as intelligent and capable people, but if it's trendy to always talk about how dumb you are or what a useless human your husband is, then you do you, babe.

I Don't Want to Be Famous

I personally don't want to be famous. I know this sounds ridiculous coming from an influencer, but it's the honest truth. Do I want to further grow my social media audience? Of course, I do. And before you think I've just unwittingly contradicted myself, let me explain how I square that circle.

I don't seek attention and I'm a fairly private person in my real life; that translates into my online life as well. I'm not someone who tells my friends when I've had a spat with my husband or if my toddler has driven me batty all day, or how much my house or latest vacation cost. So why would I tell tens of thousands of strangers, or the entire internet? To each their own, but in the engagement game of Instagram, drama and salacious personal details are what feed the machine. I guess I'm just going to need to feed it something else.

I want to grow my audience because I want to be a resource for a larger group of people for the topics that I'm passionate about, not because I'm looking for people to "fan girl" me. I also fear the lack of privacy and personal security that comes with notoriety. A fellow influencer mentioned to me that she was on a weekend getaway with her family, and someone approached them, not because she recognized the influencer, but because she recognized her children. That's a bridge too far for me.

It's a really weird feeling to be recognized by someone who follows you online. Hearing "Hey! You're Sparkle girl!" or being identified by your social media handle is a little bewildering to say the least. Maybe for me it's because I'm just an ordinary person and what you see is always what you get with me. Something I hear from almost everyone I meet in person is "You look exactly the same as you do on Instagram!" which isn't true of all influencers, I can assure you. Some are fully dolled up for the 'gram while very plain and conservative in real life.

I'm someone who receives a lot of direct messages from my audience instead of public comments and I'm okay with that. I love being able to connect with people one-on-one.

In these chats I've discussed everything from vaccination questions with nurses, to helping members of my audience choose their new kitchen backsplash tile, skincare recommendations and which baby gear I'm obsessed with.

As much as I love sharing information with a large audience, I love to have meaningful conversations with people more. Am I in the wrong profession because I don't want or care about the fame? Maybe. Or maybe not. Maybe because I'm not in it for the fame it helps me stay true to who I am and keep living my normal-girl life. Am I flattered by the attention and occasional adoration I receive? I'd be lying if I said no.

I'm also incredibly humbled by it because I'm someone who believes that we all put our pants on the same way every morning – one leg at a time.

CHAPTER 2

INFLUENCERS ARE THE NEW MEAN GIRLS

Just in case you didn't get enough mean girl drama in high school, the influencer world is here to fill that void in your life. As much as creating content is a legitimate business and as hard as so many of these women hustle, there is just as much, if not more, immature teenage drama than you're going find on a varsity cheer team.

FOMO[2], jealousy, entitlement, gossip, backstabbing, bullying, temper tantrums and everything in between…except no one stole your boyfriend (at least not yet).

What appears to be a community of friends is really just a group of mercenaries vying for their time in the spotlight.

---

[2] FOMO: acronym for "Fear Of Missing Out"

Influencer Events: Behind the Scenes

You've seen it late night scrolling through Instagram Stories: countless influencers that you know snapping photos together at a local event for a restaurant, retail store, art exhibit or anything a PR company would promote, selling you on why you need to check out your city's newest hotspot. It looks glamorous. It looks like fun. It looks like a red carpet affair for the popular girls in town who are clearly best friends...right?!

Are influencer events fun? Yes, they can be. It can be fun to be the first to check out a new space before the general public. There's something really cool about being included in this group of tastemakers, however, that's not the whole story. These events have become tired – and it's not because the PR companies are doing a poor job. It's because the drama is literally exhausting.

I have had a front-row seat to some pretty jaw-droppingly poor conduct at influencer events and I can't seem to skip an event without hearing tales of bad behavior that I missed out on witnessing firsthand.

What may appear to be a group of composed women posting quality curated content to their Instagram feeds with a smile on their face, is in all actuality a group of astoundingly insecure women battling each other to be relevant.

Why Is *She* Here?

"Ugh. Why did she even get invited? She only has X number of followers." Ah, yes. One invitee was not privy to the guest list prior to attendance and finds that her presence is somehow more or less valuable based on the others in the room. She is angry that influencers of what she deems to be of significantly lower social standing because of their comparative follower count should not be in attendance.

If someone with a fraction of her precious following is in attendance, then perhaps she should be compensated for her "appearance" because there is no way they should be considered equals or peers on a guest list. She airs her grievances *at the event* to the event hosts in less than hushed tones.

I'm not sure how tearing a PR or brand rep a new one at a public event is beneficial to your business or overall reputation, but you do you girl. Leave the rest of us out of it. We're just going to stand over here outside of the splash zone.

Here's another fun example: One of the invited influencers is angry and scorned that at an event for *influencers*, a well-known model and her team are also present and shooting promotional content for the exhibit's marketing materials. This is offensive to her as it "makes everyone feel badly to have to watch this". A normal, well-adjusted person would think that watching a model shoot content live is a cool, behind-the-scenes experience. They might also see it as a way to pick up some free pro-tips rather than a slight against their own content creation abilities.

What's interesting to note about the *Why is she here?* question is that it goes both ways. Self-entitled influencers attending these events believe that certain invites should not have been sent all while other influencers sit at home feeling excluded for not having received an invite at all. *How do you get on these magic lists? Why was she invited and not me? I love that brand – why wasn't I invited?*

I'm Sorry, Who Are You?!

Watching how influencers interact with each other can be incredibly eye opening. Seeing how some more experienced influencers interact with those who are their juniors or are considered 'up-and-coming' can be hard to watch. I once saw someone new to the industry approach a local influencer with a significantly larger following only to be met with cold reservation. The junior influencer did "fan girl" her a little bit, which you would assume she would have reacted favorably to, considering how much she loves attention from her adoring fans, but this was different.

Rather than a friendly meet-and-greet with a fan who loves her content, this situation was clearly a guarded attempt to keep anyone from displacing her. After all, no one helped her rise to the follower count status she now holds so why should she offer anyone any helpful advice. The industry is competitive and it's important for her to play her cards close.

Don't You Know Who I Am?!

I remember quite vividly attending a holiday influencer event at a big box store when I was 4 days postpartum with my first child (oh, and it was during a snowstorm, so…). But before you think I'm the crazy one in this story, keep reading.

This event was really well done, right down to the generous swag bags we were sent home with. There were in-store product demonstrations, contests and draws for us to win some pretty amazing prizes, all on top of a whole host of other goodies.

In case you aren't aware, most in-store demonstrators for brands are not directly employed by the brands themselves (i.e. like the Costco sample people!). They have no say in influencer campaigns or marketing budgets. They are only there to inform customers on the brand's product offering in as much detail as they can.

Enter the angry influencer on a warpath. PR reps and fellow influencers immediately take a deep breath and a few steps back. Some are looking for popcorn because they know a show's about to start for this influencer carries a reputation for putting on a good one.

The angry influencer approaches the in-store demonstrator and immediately blurts out: "I have emailed and emailed and emailed your company for the last year and no one has gotten back to me." Okay. Followed by: "Do you know who I am? Do you know how many followers I have on Instagram? I can't understand why your company would not get back to me to work together when I have more than twice what their other influencers have on Instagram."

Insert shell-shocked brand rep here, still saying nothing. "Your company is a big black hole when it comes to emails, so explain to me why no one has replied to me." The reply of "I'm so sorry that this has been your experience, but I have nothing to do with the departments that handle any of that" is of course met with swift disgust, more angry complaints, and a thickening of the air all around her.

Again, great for business, right? Not so much. Brand reps and PR people talk and behavior like this is noted and recorded for future campaigns. This is one of the quickest ways to get onto a brand or marketing agency's "Do Not Call" list.

General Mean Girl Behavior

It can be intimidating to attend these events, especially solo (if you aren't offered a plus one). Cliques of girls who know each other from other events, or even DMs or engagement pods, can be hard to approach. It's also really hard when you see girls that you know vehemently despise each other are laughing and carrying on as if everything is peachy. The entire experience can be really nerve wracking, especially if you're alone. They aren't necessarily the potential friendship opportunities they appear to be.

Have you ever walked up to a group of people only for them to immediately stop talking? I've attended private shopping events where pairs of women were hiding behind clothing racks whispering about other girls at the event.

Am I the influencer you think shouldn't be in attendance? Is there something on my face?

It's also uncomfortable seeing others who are there solo that you can see have been alienated from the group. It's even more anxiety-inducing when you know some of those people have been cyber-bullied by others in the room.

Sure, it can be fun to see a few familiar faces and get to know your colleagues in the influencer community, but at what cost? At some point you have to start asking yourself if it was worth the free gift card or the night out to subject yourself to this kind of misery and anxiety (and the junior high flashbacks).

CHAPTER 3

INFLUENCER FRENEMIES

Are they really friends or is it just for Instagram? Is there even a real way to tell? Has that pair had a recent falling out? They still comment on each other's posts in the same benign fashion they did before, so who can tell. Unless you were to bump into a pair or pack of influencers who were hanging out together for fun and not under the guise of filming content, then sure.

I know some influencers whose entire circle of friends is made up of other influencers. Sure, they all have that in common, but like any high school clique, there is always a perceived leader. There's one influencer who the others "fan girl" a little too hard, tag in too many of their Instagram stories and worship in her posts' comments.

To be honest, it's nice to have a few friends who are fellow influencers because it's nice to have colleagues that "get it". They understand how you feel when a brand deal didn't go through, or they share your latest post to their stories when it was under-performing, and you really wanted to impress the brand you were working with. They know what it takes to create content and hustle hard, sometimes without being taken seriously by your own friends and loved ones.

Those same friends will feel your pain when another influencer you both know got chosen for a collaboration over you.

Lies Women Tell Online

Some women genuinely seek to help other women and to lift each other up. Some experienced influencers love to mentor younger, up-and-coming influencers either out of kindness or the belief that there is enough room for everyone. Others do shout-outs to share their favorite peer accounts out of genuine love, without the expectation of a reciprocal gesture.

On the other hand, many influencers see the world of brand sponsorships as a pie, in that if someone achieves something then that must mean that there is somehow less left for them. In a world where we are trying to teach young girls to work together and collaborate, women are still just as competitive and cutthroat as ever.

This isn't the case with all influencers, of course, but it's worth noting that when influencers are willing to share brand contacts with each other that it is a conscious choice, if not calculated. It's often with influencers who are in other geographic markets or serve different demographic audiences, rather than with any other peer who asks. They will help a colleague out, but carefully, with their own interests protected first.

Because of these experiences I find statements like "Real Queens Fix Each Other's Crowns!" and the use of hashtags like these always raises suspicions:

#SquadGoals #FindYourTribe #GirlGang #WomenSupportingWomen #BabesSupportingBabes #CollaborationOverCompetition #StrongerTogether.

Seeing these hashtags **should** make me feel encouraged, rather than queasy.

Influencer vs. Influencer

There isn't a single group of people out there who keep tabs on influencers like other influencers do. It's almost startling to see this group watching each other's every move as if their personal statistics were on a perpetual leaderboard in an infinite competition.

Here is just a snippet of DMs I've received from influencers about other influencers:

How is she getting that product collaboration?
That collab makes absolutely no sense for her brand.
Do you think her likes are real? Do you think she pads her stats?
Every one of her posts is a collaboration – she has no other content on her feed.
She hasn't posted in weeks because she hasn't had any paid collabs.
That collab looked really good – do you think I should reach out to that brand?
How does she get so many collabs when her photos aren't even that good?
Did you see her almost lack of caption for that collab – the brand must be pissed! It's like she didn't even try.

This is just scratching the surface and these messages are only about the influencer business, not the influencers themselves. These messages don't even begin to address the mom-shaming, parenting comments, remarks on physical appearances, questions about income levels and affordability of lifestyle…you name it, I've heard it. And don't worry – I'll talk about some of these later!

The problem with this constant watching is that it can turn into an obsession that borders into the territory of mental illness in the form of addiction. One influencer shared with me that her husband does not allow her to log in to Instagram on the weekends because he believes this obsession has taken over her life and has caused her to neglect her family. It's one thing to scope out the competition to get a sense of where you can grow your own business. It's another thing investing so much time monitoring what your peer group is and isn't doing that it becomes entirely counterproductive, not to mention the personal toll that it takes on your relationships.

Do you obsess over every detail of the life of the accountant in the next cubicle? I sure hope not. I'm confident that your "workplace proximity associate" doesn't share countless details of their personal life on the company bulletin board. And even if they did, would you care how many other people cared about it? It's definitely food for thought.

The Support is Real...But Only If It's Reciprocal

Influencers comment heavily on each other's Instagram posts because they all know that they need to engage with others to get engagement on their own posts. It's a social network, after all, and influencers require engagement to impress brands so that they can land more paid collaborations. But not all influencers seem to follow this social contract, at least not without the push of an engagement pod that is moderated (more on this later).

Sometimes it doesn't matter how much you engage on someone's posts, they won't reciprocate. Influencers "target" their engagement by regularly commenting on the posts of established accounts in the hopes that those accounts (and their followers) will eventually engage back with them, all with the goal of boosting their own metrics.

This targeting doesn't always work and it's understandable when the person you are engaging with is a busy celebrity, or a regular person who isn't privy to the concept that it's just a strategy to get them to engage back, rather than because you genuinely like their content. It's extra frustrating when this happens between influencers because as an influencer, you are supposed to be aware of this unwritten rule that "if I scratch your back, you scratch mine".

She stopped engaging on my posts so to hell with her. If an influencer stops engaging back on posts, the consequences can be more dire than a simple loss of engagement from those accounts. Other influencers will hold grudges. Unless you have a good reason to have not re-engaged or at least responded to the comments left on your posts by your colleagues, you can expect a cold shoulder at the next event. That's right – you'll see pairs or small groups of influencers whispering to one another in seemingly important conversations, so much so that your mere presence can't even be acknowledged.

Muting is King

Are there influencers that I don't like? Yes. Are there influencers whose content used to clutter my feed and annoy me with their every post? Yes. But some of these influencers are people that I encounter in real life, *in person,* and cannot unfollow for that reason. The introduction of Instagram's "mute" feature is the best of both worlds that solves this problem for everyone.

The tool allows users to keep following those accounts that annoy them, or make them feel "less than", from showing up in their feed without making them look like a jerk for unfollowing a local colleague or vengeful fellow influencer. If you're reading that thinking it's disingenuous, consider how many of your annoying relative sharing every second of their day on Facebook that you've muted (because their mom will call your mom if you block or unfriend them) and you'll understand what I mean.

The Unfollow Says It All

Influencers can mute one another, they can stop engaging on each other's content, but nothing says "you're dead to me" than hitting the unfollow button. Of course, there are influencers who will see that another influencer isn't following them back and that will prompt them to immediately *unfollow* in what seems like some sort of retaliatory act, but this isn't the banality that I'm referring to.

It often takes some sort of unspeakable action to drive members of a community to go this far. And there is no gossip that spreads through the influencer community faster than "Did you see that they unfollowed each other? Like, what happened? I thought they were *best* friends!" It also doesn't take long to see who else unfollowed either side in solidarity.

I have had a falling out with another influencer and neither of us have unfollowed the other. I'm sure we've both muted one another (or maybe she hasn't muted me, who knows?). We don't engage on each other's posts, but we still follow each other. I have no real reason to follow or unfollow her and so I've left it at the status quo.

Like Taylor Swift says: "I forgot that you existed. It isn't love, it isn't hate. It's just indifference."[3]

---

[3] Taylor Swift song entitled "I Forgot That You Existed" from Lover (2019)

CHAPTER 4

BRAND IDENTITY: LIFESTYLE OR DRAMA

Influencers can be known for a variety of brand identities and can see their popularity rise through a number of means. When someone becomes an influencer, it is usually because they've started an Instagram account that has found reasonable success based on their voice on a certain topic like mom life, home décor, DIYs, fashion, etc. But just because they started in one niche doesn't mean that's where they'll stay – especially if they're chasing the money.

Many influencers showcase a lifestyle that is equal parts relatable and inspiring to their audiences. It's "relatable" because audiences tend to follow someone that they see a little bit of themselves in, but also inspires them to up their game with something like the newest baby gear or a gorgeous new area rug.

They love that influencer's lifestyle and want to emulate it in their own lives.

What is a "Lifestyle Influencer" Anyway?

Lifestyle is defined by the Oxford Dictionary as "the way in which a person or group lives". It goes on to define the term as a "way of life", a "situation", or "position" and "denoting advertising of products designed to appeal to a consumer by association with a desirable lifestyle". Interesting. Can't shake the advertising bit.

Every influencer worth her financial weight knows that some product niches and brand identities carry with them more earning opportunities than others. Most influencers dub themselves as "Lifestyle Influencers" because they literally share their personal "lifestyle". This title allows them to dabble in a little bit of everything; translation: they are just diversifying their content portfolio to make as much money as possible.

Being in the lifestyle space means that an influencer can peddle toys for the holidays (yay to free Christmas gifts!), post photos in outerwear (to put clothes on their kids' backs), share their favorite recipes (hello, meal delivery services or a new electric mixer!) or share parts of their home (because who doesn't need a free mattress or set of dishes?!).

What a Lifestyle Influencer should do: Simply adds products that they use or have in their homes to their organic Instagram feed of photos about their lives. Their captions should be captivating and helpful, offering advice or sharing something interesting about them.

This of course speaks to the origins of the industry: regular people sharing the things they use and love in an organic way because they are genuinely enthusiastic about those things. These posts sharing what they love fit seamlessly into a feed of authentic moments captured in photos.

What a Lifestyle Influencer seems to do: Peddles every product under the sun, whether they *actually* use it or just pretend to, in an Instagram feed that is made up of staged photos with banal captions. Most of the time you will see a feed full of only sponsored ads where their family and homes are the models, or rather props, in each post.

This is the direction that the industry seems to be headed: the simple selling of ad space on a social media feed, relevant or not. Posts full of brand talking points with no authentic voice or even clues as to whether the person posting even believes the message they're selling.

Your Brand is Drama

Something that can be wonderful about social media is the ability to make others feel seen. Sharing a deeply personal story and connecting with an audience can be an incredible thing, but it's a fine line to walk. We've all had that friend whose call we've sent to voicemail because we can't listen to them complain about their problems anymore. We can't listen to whatever childhood trauma they are still holding onto in their 30s for the umpteenth time. The same goes for influencers.

A friend asks you, "Did you see what *Unnamed Influencer* posted today?" to which you would reply with the question, "Which one is *she* again?"

The answers are any or all that follow:

- "The one who always talks about how much sex she and her husband are having."
- "The one who always talks about how poor they are but has sponsored posts for expensive stuff."
- "She's the mom-blogger who only posts photos of her kids." "Which blogger?" "I don't know, there are so many now!"
- "The one whose feed is a highlight reel of breastfeeding photos."
- "The one who used to talk about travel but now her stories are all anti-vax conspiracies."
- "The one who went through that messy divorce last year and posted every detail."

33

- "The one who keeps posting photos of her stretch marks."
- "The one who is always depressed all the time, even though her life looks amazing."
- "The one who always talks about how they had to go to marriage counseling. Sounds like her husband is an a-hole."
- "The one whose kid is always in the hospital for some reason or another."
- "The one who all she talks about is her ill/unalive child and posts those unsettling photos of horrifying moments."
- "You know, the one who only talks about how she was sexually assaulted."

Talk about one thing too much and that's and all people will remember you for. It defines your brand whether you like it or not. The drama that influencers share from their lives is a great way to drum up engagement – everyone loves to watch a dumpster fire, but if that's all an influencer shared for a considerable amount of time, that's all they'll be remembered for.

"Did you see the stretch mark girl is peddling cough medicine this week?" Yeah. What's her handle? No one entirely remembers. What's her brand? That she has apparently has a lot of stretch marks.

Rather than sharing the occasional personal story from their journey, influencers get caught up in the dramatic overshare and are addicted to the likes, engagement, and temporary notoriety that comes with it. It's one thing to be authentic and vulnerable with your audience, but it is quite another for that to be your entire brand and the only thing you post about.

If your kid has a terminal illness and that's all you share, but somehow with some sponsored brand collaborations sprinkled in, it's going to be hard for people to take you seriously. Their followers are interested in the story and want to offer support and compassion but feel a little bewildered when you're trying to sell them something in between photos of their kid in a hospital bed.

I want to be clear: I'm not saying that sharing a personal story of assault or the journey of infertility is only to drum up sales and draw the eyes of more followers. I'm not saying that every feed that shares photos of a deceased child on their deathbed is for sympathy or attention because sometimes it is to raise awareness about a rare disease that needs our attention. I'm not body shaming someone who is trying to help normalize what bearing children does to change most women's bodies. It's quite the opposite.

I applaud those who are willing to share their personal stories so that others in the world feel "seen"; showing others that life isn't always picture-perfect and that influencers are real people, too. Sometimes being such a "real" person is what grew their audience in the first place, and that's a great thing.

Unfortunately, one of the many problems with this is that many users neglect to read captions. Perhaps all of these posts of breastfeeding or stretch marks or of an influencer in their underwear for the zillionth time tell a story, a story that is in the caption that has gone unread. At some point the images on their feed will start to be white noise, no matter how dramatic or shocking they appear.

For me, the drama doesn't sell me and it doesn't draw me in. I've had to mute a number of accounts that I follow for various reasons. I couldn't handle the energy of seeing babies attached to tubes or a photoshoot of a child's dying moments on my feed while I was pregnant, or honestly in general.

I don't want to know how a stranger's marriage counselling is going; I wish them well, but I don't want to be invited into their marriage and their quarrels with one another because I feel like it's none of my business - and please stop trying to make it my business because you're using that to build yours.

I didn't invite a camera crew into the delivery room when I gave birth and if "dog forbid" someone close to me were to pass away, I wouldn't invite hired paparazzi to document that moment either.

Often those influencers will start to see a lot of people hit the "unfollow" button because once the drama is gone, the audience has moved on to the next saga.

CHAPTER 5

THE AUTHENTICITY GAP

The biggest issue that I see in influencer marketing is what I like to call "The Authenticity Gap". People don't trust influencers anymore, and it's not hard to see why. But just in case it is, I'm going to take a deep dive into it here for you.

In discussing what is causing the general public to distrust influencers, and for many in their audiences to hit the "unfollow" button, I think it's important to realize how we got here. What used to be considered "the new word of mouth" is now a group of vapid nobodies selling themselves to the highest bidder with no regard for authenticity because, for most of them, it doesn't matter anymore. It doesn't matter if you like something or not, someone is paying you really good money to pretend that you do.

I want to make it clear that when I'm speaking about authenticity, particularly in this chapter, that I'm not talking about the authenticity of followers or engagement, but rather about the influencers themselves. It's also important to be clear that there is still a group of creators out there who are very discerning about the projects they take on and the brands that they endorse, but I believe that group is in the minority.

How To Go from Selling to Sell-Out

What originally made influencer marketing feel so organic and special was its authenticity. Influencers were sharing products that they loved in a really genuine way – *actually* genuine because they weren't being paid to do it (yet) and even *more* genuine because they were sharing their message with audiences that they had built organically over time.

It was before brands realized how powerful these social media personalities were; before they started devoting significant marketing budgets to paying them for content and endorsements. It was before there was a race for everyone to be "Insta-famous" just for the fame and free stuff; before influencers had to disclose when they were paid to endorse a product with #AD, #GIFTED or #SPONSORED.

Before influencer marketing had its name, every day people were following strangers on the internet that they felt connected to or inspired by. They would follow these accounts because they loved someone's personal style or home décor aesthetic or the recipes they shared – or in the case of a "lifestyle influencer" all the above. Maybe they were a travel lover, so following a real person on their vacation made the trip they were dreaming of seem more accessible than reading about it in *Conde Nast*.

Following someone who was close to your age, in what felt like a similar life stage and on likely the same budget as you was inspiring and maybe a bit comforting, too. You felt like you had a "friend" of sorts that shared all the best stuff with you.

Then somewhere along the line, the influencer that you felt so connected to, the person you felt like was your online buddy whose life you followed from a safe but interested distance, started selling to you. They realized the power and monetization capabilities of their 'influence' – and so did brands.

First it was products that made sense to you. After all, you always wondered where she got those cute jeans and you didn't want to seem like a creep asking her what skincare she used to keep that continuous glow she always seemed to have. And so, it was cool that she was sharing the details. Then it was a new mattress, which I guess makes sense, because she just re-designed her bedroom. You thought *I bet she did her research, too – that's why she chose this mattress!* not realizing that maybe that was the only mattress company that said yes to working with her.

Then she started sharing fast food restaurants which felt a little odd considering those delicious homemade recipes she used to share. *Thoughtful pause.*

Then it was extravagant hotel stays that you wouldn't be able to afford but didn't think *she could* either. Her similar budget was what made you feel connected to her in the first place, and why you loved following her for her amazing suggestions and ideas. You're, of course, happy for her for her success, but now you feel like the person who was once offering you options that you could afford on your budget, too, now seems like she's on another level and she has left you behind.

The cute jeans she's sharing cost 5x the ones she used to share – and that glowing skin? It's not from the numerous skincare brands she claims to use, but from the injectables clinic she just started working with. Her captions used to be clever and inspiring. You felt like you knew her and were connected to her somehow, but now they're just empty with what seem like effortless attempts to sell you things with quips like "What's cuter? Me or these dishes?!" or "Use this code so I can get some taco money." instead of her sharing why these dishes were either worth the splurge or gorgeous despite their budget-friendly price point. *Click to unfollow.*

Some influencers are so busy with brand work that their feeds scroll like a constant ad-reel. Each post, one after another, selling a different product every day of the week. I've even seen some influencers post photos between sponsored content with captions like "Filler Pic" as if to say *"I have nothing of value to say if I'm not trying to sell you something, but I needed to break up my feed, so here it is."* Wow, thanks for that waste of time. I'm scrolling through my social media looking for content that is supposed to inspire me or make me feel connected to the online community, but "filler pic" tells me exactly where we stand. ***Click to unfollow.***

If an influencer is starting to lose their value with their own audience, they must be losing value with brands, too, right? Yes and no. If an influencer is getting a ton of brand deals, that usually snowballs into more brand deals, not less. More and more deals can make an influencer look like the "It Girl" du-jour and brands want a piece of it, just like everyone else does.

No One Can LOVE That Many Things *(At the Same Time)*

Now it's not to say that all brands are this way. Some brands have stopped working with influencers whose feeds they deem to be too saturated with ad content for fear that their placement will get lost in what is now just white noise to audiences. Something I'm asked more often than people realize by those outside of the influencer marketing industry is *"Can anyone really like **that** many things? Like, how many brands of (insert product type here) do you actually like?"*

Audiences see influencers peddling product after product in the same category and are beginning to question the authenticity of it all. And rightfully so!

Brands are getting wise to this, too, asking influencers for non-compete clauses in contracts to ensure that the influencer doesn't endorse a similar product within a certain time frame. This sounds like something that an authentic influencer should be doing on their own, but the truth is, they aren't because it's a paycheck.

I've watched influencers post three different anti-aging skin care brands in the same week, and not in the context of *"I've reviewed these three brands and here's what I think of each"* but rather in three separate paid endorsements for something you should consider buying. Does anyone really love *three* different skin care routines that do the exact same thing? Be honest with yourself here. Oh, and those non-compete clauses? Yeah, about that. Business-savvy influencers charge extra for those, so that's not as authentic as you think it is either.

Fit For Authenticity

Some brands and the PR firms who rep them are becoming a lot more discerning about who they choose to work with, too. They do their research on not only the content, but also on the size and demographic reach that an influencer has, for overall fit. A vegan blogger shouldn't be peddling turkey bacon and someone with school-aged children shouldn't be endorsing the newest innovation in diapers. This is usually what happens, but sometimes brands just throw a bunch of money at the wall (of influencers) in a big media blast regardless of fit or logic. That's usually when you see every influencer on your feed pushing the same product within a week.

"Fit" is something that I've seen upset influencers. For instance, a very high-end department store opened a new location in our city and the influencer community was abuzz with excitement. One fashion blogger with a larger following than most of her local peers found herself left off the list for the store's opening events and was very disgruntled as to why. A casual observer familiar with this influencer and her brand would assume that she wasn't invited because her feed was a constant endorsement of discount stores, inexpensive fast fashion, drugstore cosmetic brands and collaborations with big box stores like Wal-Mart.

This isn't exactly the right fit for a store that sells high-end fashion and cosmetics, catering to an elite group of customers in a very high-income bracket.

The Opposite Effect/Intent of Influencer Marketing

There are some fellow influencers that I've followed but always kind of felt like they were a bit, for lack of better term: *trashy*, just based on their overall vibe, how they speak to their audience and stuff like that. Then I saw them work with some brands that I really loved but felt like were *higher-end* and I had to wonder if those brands were really for me anymore.

A specific example that comes to mind is an influencer who often referred to herself as "poor" and made frequent mention to her inability to afford things for herself or her family. She then did a campaign talking about the amazing personal shopping services available at a high-end department store. Hmm. I can't decide who is more inauthentic in this situation: Is it the influencer or the brand?

Authenticity is Everything (To Me)

I've written a few sponsored Instagram captions and even blog posts where I was baring my soul when sharing why a product was so impactful to my life. I struggled with breastfeeding with my first born. I ended up using the *BabyBrezza Formula Pro* machine, which I endorsed because it really did make a difference in my life. After struggling even more so with breastfeeding after the birth of my second child, which I believe is worth noting that it was my second child in less than two years, this machine was a godsend that I felt like I couldn't live without.

To top it all off, I felt a lot of shame for not being able to breastfeed and nourish either of my babies. Especially with all of the photos posted by other influencers on Instagram of their child latched to their breast with captions like "This is pure magic!" or "Breast is best – let's spread the message of how important this is!" or "There is no better way to bond with your baby."

Maybe it was that I hit my breaking point and I just couldn't take the shame that social media was making me feel over and over again when I had two perfectly fed and healthy baby girls. Maybe it was that I knew I couldn't be the only mother out there who felt like she was in over her head in the depths of postpartum and a machine, *yes a machine*, changed my life and made my life so much easier than anyone could ever imagine and so I not only wanted, but felt like I *needed* to share my story.

Was it a sponsored post? Yes. But in posting my editorial titled *Shame, Thy Name is Bottle Feeding (My Breastfeeding Journeys...or Lack Thereof)* it wasn't so much about pushing a product that I would never want to live without, but rather it was about making other women feel seen.

Now, I know I can't do that with every product that I share on my Instagram feed. Few products have impacted my life like this one did, and I don't think I could have the same passion about the gummy vitamins that I take as I could for this, and rightfully so. But you see the point I'm making here.

I'm Fiercely Brand Loyal and Always Have Been

One of the reasons I started blogging and ended up in the world of influencer marketing is because I naturally recommend products that I love to strangers. If I see you debating the purchase of an item at Costco and I have purchased said item and love it, I will approach you and give you my unsolicited opinion and endorsement of that product because I can't help myself. I've been this way my whole life.

I'm also someone who very much knows what she wants. When I was pregnant with my first child, I knew exactly which stroller I wanted. I was approached by a few different stroller companies and politely passed while I waited to hear back from the stroller brand I wanted. If that brand had declined to work with me, I may have tried to work with them through a distributor, but if in turn that still didn't materialize, I would have just bought the stroller outright, rather than take one of the others offered to me.

I didn't want to settle. I'd rather buy the stroller that I wanted and not bother with a direct endorsement of it (in a dedicated social media post) than settle for another stroller that wasn't everything I wanted. I realize that this sounds a little bit privileged, but the point I'm trying to make here is about not selling out and I'm about to tell you why.

The Regret and Shame of Selling Out

I bet you're wondering if I've ever crossed that line, and you're reading this thinking *Oh, come on, Carlee. Like you've never endorsed something you didn't 100% love because the money was good?* And you would be exactly right. I have.

I still look back on it feeling kind of gross. Every time I see that brand in a store, I feel guilty. Early on in my influencer career, the idea of getting paid for posting was still a bit novel to me and every time a brand approached me, I felt like it was an opportunity to prove to myself (and others) that I should be taken seriously (yes, I see the irony). After all, a brand was *paying* me so I must be doing something right. In this case, I was being paid to recommend a bottle of pretty inexpensive (*okay fine I'll say it, cheap*) wine and I did it.

If you follow me on social or read my blog, you know that my love of wine is a big part of my life and in turn, my brand. I love wine so much that it led me to pursue my Level 2 Sommelier Certification, so when I recommend a wine, I take it *really* seriously. I think that's what made this feel all the more icky.

I was paid to endorse a wine that I'd never purchased and quite honestly, don't really like. It's not a brand I would buy unless I knew someone expressly loved this bottle so much that I knew I couldn't offer them something else.

I know it was a paycheck (it wasn't even that much money) and I should just move on, but it still haunts me: the shame of it. If I told you to go out and buy this not-so-great bottle of wine to enjoy on a Friday night, then why would you trust me when I tell you that I love my mattress or my stroller or my *(insert any other product here)*?

What am I if I don't have my integrity and how useful am I at "influencing" if I'm just peddling whatever comes my way because *hey, this is how I feed my family*?

For me, this was a turning point. From that day on, I would only endorse brands that I expressly loved and if it was a product that was new to me, I had to be able to try it before agreeing to the terms of the contract.

I know I sound pretty self-righteous here but I'm not a good liar and I don't do well with deceit. I've met some of my audience members in-person and they've asked me about products that I've endorsed, and I have to be able to look them in the eye and tell them the truth.

But it's about more than that to me. At some point, peddling the product of the day on Instagram starts to feel a little bit hollow, so it I'm going to take the time and effort to produce content to sell something, it better be something worthwhile.

I don't know if it would surprise you at this point to learn how many incoming messages I receive from members of my audience asking things like:

"I've been considering this product for a while and saw your endorsed it – do you actually like it or was it just a paid gig?"

Yes, that's right!

If your audience member is bold enough, they'll come right out and ask if you *actually* like something before they buy it. But then again, how authentic is it if you reply with *"Of course I totally love it – use my promo code please!"*

Because who couldn't use some extra taco money, right?

CHAPTER 6

THE HUSTLE IS REAL

A few months ago, a family friend of mine posted something on Facebook that sent me reeling. The gist of the post was that traditional professions such as doctor, lawyer, nurse, teacher, airline pilots, etc. require years of education and professional training, whereas all you need to be a successful "influencer" is a camera and an internet connection. Hmm. Thanks, bud.

I felt incredibly disrespected and dismissed for what I do, but then I realized that this person didn't mean any harm, they were just ignorant. Seriously, just plain ignorant. Trying to get someone to take you seriously as a social media influencer and content creator (a title we'll discuss in the next chapter) is no easy feat. There are loads of misconceptions about this business – and yes, it is very much a business.

It's a business because I make money doing it. "How do you make money?" is one of the rudest, yet the most commonly asked question I have been asked since starting to blog and create content for social media. It's rude because no one asks a nurse or lawyer or electrician how they make money but being an "influencer" is such a new and extraordinary (in the most literal sense of the word) job title that people ask out of pure interest and fascination, not because they're trying to be rude. Influencers are like pseudo-celebrities and what they do is incredibly interesting to onlookers.

So, how *do* influencers make money and start working with all of these brands? Let me tell you. It sounds simple, but the hustle is real.

The Follower Count Entitlement Fallacy (or commonly called "The Brands Are Going to Come Running to Me" illusion)

There's a growing misconception that if you have a certain number of Instagram followers that brands just start magically sending you gifts in the mail and offering you money to promote them. Although this is sometimes true, because it does happen that brand reps will come across your profile and reach out because they think you're a great fit for an upcoming campaign, this isn't how most brand deals are done.

What's interesting is that there are quite a few smaller players in the influencer space who believe that all that matters is their follower count and that once they hit a certain threshold, the brands are going to come running. If you're famous for something relevant or appeared on a season of any show in ABC's *Bachelor* franchise, then sure. If you're just a basic nobody like most of us, then you're going to have to hustle your backside off to get business.

Most brand deals are made by influencers "pitching" to brands. A "pitch" is really just a cold call, or nowadays an email or direct message, that influencers send to a brand asking to work with them. And just like in commission sales, pitching is a numbers game. You want to land 5 brand deals this month? Better pitch to 10, 20, maybe even 50 brands. Very few influencers hear back from every pitch email they send, and if they do hear back, it doesn't always turn into a collaboration right away, if even at all.

Sometimes it feels like you're sending emails into the dark abyss. Other times it takes weeks and/or a few follow up emails to get a response. Sometimes your message is passed through a series of people until it reaches the correct contact person. Some brand deals are signed, posted and completed within weeks, whereas others take months, or close to a full year, to complete from pitch to post. No brand deal is ever alike.

I bet at this point you're thinking "It sounds like you just email and DM people all day asking them to give you money and products so that you can post about it on your blog and social media feeds." Yep. You're reading that correctly. And if your next thought is: "What qualifies you to ask for these things?" Well, I'm glad you asked!

Access & Influence: What a Brand is *Really* Paying For

What brands are really paying influencers for is content creation and direct access to an audience of people through someone they already know, trust, and admire. Brands could run expensive print ads in magazines with celebrities or well-known models or they could pay a social media influencer to create content for their own channels to market directly to the audience they're looking to target. Brands are paying influencers for access to the consumer: YOU.

You already follow an influencer because you like something about them; their content, personality, anything really. So do most of the other people that follow that influencer, so much so that they have built up an audience of perhaps tens of thousands of people.

Brands see a lot of value in putting a series of, in relative terms, small budgets into a group of individuals to access who they believe is their target demographic via a deemed "trusted source". The Instagram account of an influencer is just a collage of paid ad space, no different than commercial breaks on television or radio. These squares serve as semi-concealed advertisements between other potentially relevant content on a curated feed. The action of thumb scrolling has replaced the act of flipping through the pages of a print magazine.

Why Influencers Pitch to Brands

Instagram influencers are also a dime a dozen, so to stand out and differentiate yourself from the crowd, you have to introduce yourself to brands so they know who you are and that you're available to them. There are a million other accounts just like yours out there, so waiting for a brand to stumble upon your account, especially often enough to make you the equivalent income of a full-time job, is in a few words: lazy, entitled, and laughable.

It's like going to a shopping mall every day hoping for a talent agency to "discover" you. Announcing a pregnancy on Instagram and creating a registry at buybuy BABY might be enough to prompt P&G to send you diaper coupons in the mail. It's not enough to signal to stroller companies that you want to collaborate with them.

The (Un)Qualified Expert

DMs people send me: "Did you see that she's now calling herself an Instagram expert?" "When did she move into the fashion blogger space?" "How did she become an interior designer? Is she really an expert?" "Who decided that she was an "expert" in anything?"

The honest answer is *she* decided that she is an expert in XYZ.

The beauty of being an influencer is that you can call yourself an expert in any field and your adoring fans will believe you…generally speaking. When marketing budgets dried up in Q2 of 2020 due to the pandemic, many influencers sought to create and sell e-books and online courses in whatever they decided they could call dub themselves an authority. This determined who had an audience that took them seriously when it came to *actual* advice, and who did not. I say this only because not every influencer was able to convert their expertise into sales.

But that's what influencers do. We brand ourselves as an expert in *something* – even if that something is our *own* lifestyle that we're sharing.

Why Can't You Just Do It for The Free Stuff

So many brands, especially small businesses, want influencers to promote their products in exchange for product "in-kind" rather than in exchange for cash payment. For bigger ticket items this could be a reasonable offer, but for everyday products like laundry detergent or even a sweater, the time investment just isn't worth it.

There are many influencers out there who just do this for the free stuff – and that's great for them. But most influencers do this for the money for no other reason than because it's their full-time job. The barter economy of product in-kind is great, but the end of the day, you can't pay your mortgage with skin care products. You can't buy groceries with sweaters, and you can't put gas in your car with scrunchies or lipstick. Would a magazine ask an advertising agency to create print ads for them in exchange for products? And oh, maybe a discount code for their subscribers? No, they would not.

Let me quote from my DMs to share some of my favorite lowball offers:

"Can you do three posts to your Instagram feed? I'll send you two scrunchies."

Um, are these scrunchies made of gold?

"We would love to offer you a 30% discount on our clothing in exchange for three posts on your feed. We will provide a 10% off coupon for your followers."

So, you want me to buy your products at a small discount, in order to promote them, and take up three squares on my feed?

"Our generous influencer program offers you two free pieces of clothing in exchange for one feed post."

Your clothing retails for $40 per piece, so for $80 worth of product (retail), you want me to share this on my Instagram feed?

If reading these comments makes you think that I sound entitled, I promise you I'm not. The amount of time and effort that goes into creating content is not as simple as it would appear so I'm going to share that next!

CHAPTER 7

THE JACK OR JILL OF ALL TRADES...
AND THEN SOME

Now that you know what goes in to actually landing a brand deal (i.e. getting business), let's talk about the work that goes into creating the content itself. There are so many misconceptions about this out there and no matter how inauthentic the influencer personality may be, their content creation game needs to be on point, because you can't fake that.

Let's go back to the Facebook post I referenced that stated that all you need to do this job is a camera and an internet connection. It isn't as simple as snapping a quick photo on your iPhone, choosing a filter, typing up *"OMG, I loveeeeeeeee thisssssssssss"* in a caption, adding some meaningless hashtags and hitting post. That may have been the case in the early days of Instagram, but it certainly isn't anymore, and the skillset required only keeps growing.

Social media influencers have now started calling themselves "creators" and "entrepreneurs" and that's for good reason. It isn't a matter of political correctness or euphemism either. This isn't a "stewardess" asking to be called a "flight attendant" or a "gas jockey" suddenly asking for the title of "petroleum transfer engineer". Influencers are independent business owners who create content for brands and agencies on a freelance basis for commission.

Think of everything that a brand used to pay a traditional advertising agency for, things like print ads or even television commercials, and then put it into the context of a social media influencer creating this content for them, from start to finish. Brands are paying for access to an influencer's audience of followers, but they're also paying them for the content used to sell to that audience, and potentially use it in their own advertising campaigns.

The Ever-Changing Environment of Social Media

Social media is something that continues to evolve and for those who create content for it, especially paid marketing content, must evolve with it. Ignoring other social media platforms and just focusing on Instagram specifically, and how it has evolved, is enough to make your head spin as a consumer, let alone a creator.

What started as a simple photo sharing app eventually added Stories (because who needs SnapChat anymore?). Then came the longer-format vertical videos of IGTV (so bye-bye, Vine). And then came Reels (because TikTok's popularity was hard to ignore). This means that there are three forms of content that you need to master creating in order to keep up with what brands are asking for – on just one platform alone.

Let's Talk About Skills, Baby!

The list of skills required to be a social media influencer, or at least a financially successful one, is long. It also comes with a necessary list of equipment and computer software to get it right, too. If anything, being a social media influencer is a good resume builder of often self-taught skills.

In the simplest terms, an influencer must be a master photographer and videographer all while also having a keen grasp of the Adobe Creative Suite (or something like it). Oh, and they must have a firm understanding of contract law and accounting while being a great salesperson and expert negotiator. I should also mention set designer, fashion consultant, prop master, graphic designer and overall administrator and record keeper. All while being cheerful and positive and having a smile on their face.

Let me break it all down for you.

Skill Required: Photography & Photo Editing

I'm sure these ones seem pretty obvious considering photos are the bulk of what influencers post but remember: it's not as simple as snapping a quick pic on your phone. Most brands request that content be shot with a DSLR Camera in high resolution. Depending on available photoshoot location options, additional lighting may be required. These photos must then be edited to ensure proper lighting, aesthetic, and tone (hello, Adobe Lightroom!).

But let's take it back a step. The influencer must first conceptualize the photo and style for not only the "set" where the photo is being taken, but also add any necessary props to execute the proper aesthetic. They must also take the appropriate steps to ensure that they themselves match the visual appeal required for the photo. Translation: Glam. #WokeUpLikeThis doesn't work here. Hair, makeup, and the right outfit all matter when trying to execute a single photo…and that isn't a five-minute job either.

Skill Required: Videography & Video Editing

These skills don't differ much from those listed above but add in the extra conditions required to shoot a video. Instagram Reels aren't usually shot with a DSLR, but to get the quality most brands are looking for influencers usually need one of the most recent iPhone (or equivalent) models. And not all videos can be edited that easily on a smartphone, even with third party apps, so for those television commercial-worthy Instagram Reels that you see, they've been edited with software like Adobe Premiere.

So far the jobs I have listed include Photographer, Videographer, Editor, Creative Director, Set Designer & Lighting Consultant, Prop Master, Costume Designer, Hair and Makeup Artist. It's like you need a Bachelor of Fine Arts just to take a single photo for Instagram and I haven't even scratched the surface of the list of skills required to be successful at this!

Skill Required: Copy Writer

Some influencers really lack skill in the copy writing department, but they often make up for it with being witty or clever. As much as I believe that spelling and grammar count in the real world, they don't seem to matter to many influencers out there. Regardless of my feelings on this or my desire to get up on a linguistic soap box, being able to write well enough to connect with people on a semi-regular basis is a job requirement, nonetheless.

There are some in the industry who openly state that they don't proofread because it's "more authentic that way". Great, I'm glad that your third grade writing abilities are shining through, authentically.

Skill Required: Research, Relationship Building & Administration

There is often a great deal of research that goes in to finding the correct contact person and email address for a brand that an influencer wants to work with. Sometimes this information is readily available on a brand's website, but quite often it can take some digging.

Influencers also must actively maintain relationships with a variety of PR firms and advertising agencies that represent large numbers of brands, managing their advertising campaigns and budgets. All good influencers keep a list of who these key people are, and know when they move to other brands or firms in the industry. At the end of the day, this is a people business, and established relationships go a long way to continuing to be considered for paid work.

Skill Required: Graphic Designer

When an influencer approaches a brand, just like applying for any other job, a resume of sorts is required. In influencer terms, what is sent over is called a "Media Kit" or "Press Kit". This is a 1-5 page document that gives a brief introduction and biography of the influencer, lists the metrics and demographic reach of their social media channels and/or blog, as well as a brief list or highlight reel of brands the influencer has worked with in the past. This is of course all in a document that has to look pretty and on-brand.

For social media content, especially for any non-basic Instagram story or collage post that you see on someone's feed, there is some graphic design component required. If an influencer has a blog or is on a platform like Pinterest, the need for quality graphics is non-negotiable. Even a banner on a Facebook Page or Twitter profile require graphic design skills.

Skill Required: Sales & Negotiation

Almost every pitch email sent to a brand is a cold sales call. It's usually called a "pitch" because it's a quick "elevator pitch" that quickly summarizes who an influencer is and how/why they want to work with a brand. Once an influencer begins discussions with a brand (who is really a potential client) then negotiations begin. Even if a brand reaches out to an influencer, the negotiation process still has to take place.

Advertising budgets, content scope and project rates are all discussed here. An influencer not only has to sell themselves to a brand to sign a contract with them, but they also must know how to successfully sell to their own audience in the content that they create.

Skill Required: Planning & Logistics

An influencer's content calendar can be tricky to manage. If you're sarcastically thinking "Yeah, must be *so* hard to figure out when I'm going to post about all this amazing free stuff", you would be very wrong. Some brands have very, very specific go-live dates for their advertising campaigns and some are now asking that their sponsored post not fall within a certain number of hours or days of other sponsored content. Even unsponsored content is still carefully planned out in advance to ensure that it provides the right amount of spacing between sponsored posts.

Skill Required: Contract Negotiation

Very few brand deals are done with a virtual handshake anymore, so an influencer needs to know the ins and outs of contract law and its associated terminology. It's not just important to understand the terms of a contract to know what you need to post or what the content approval and posting deadlines are – there are more clauses being added all the time.

Content usage rights and ownership, whitelisting, how long an influencer must leave a post on their feed before deleting or archiving, exclusivity rights...and the very boring but important list goes on.

Skill Required: Accounting

Brands don't just magically send influencers money after a job well done. They are most often major corporations and require an influencer to send them an invoice to be paid – and it's up to the influencer to keep up on their accounts receivable, too, to ensure they get paid on time. Oh, and because this *is* a business, an influencer must be up on what expenses they can and can't deduct when filing their own taxes at the end of the year.

Skill Required: Personality

It was easier for influencer to get away with being fairly "flat" in the personality department when Instagram was just a photo sharing app. Now that the platform, and in turn brands, require live Stories and other video content where an influencer speaks directly to their audience, an influencer always has to be on their game. It's a lot easier to hide (or edit!) how tired you are in a still photo than it is in a video.

So why do creators charge so much for the work that they do?

I have a feeling the list above clears up a lot of the mystery associated with that. Consider that almost all of the skills that I've just listed are required for each and every contract an influencer signs.

It also bears mentioning how expensive some of the equipment and software needed can be. Upgrading cameras, purchasing new lenses, a quality computer that can handle the software requirements add up to thousands of dollars in up-front expenses.

I bet that you'll stop your scroll and think a little harder about the next sponsored post you see on Instagram.

CHAPTER 8

INSTAGRAM VS. REALITY

Instagram isn't real. I honestly hope that this statement didn't just blow your mind and shatter your world view, but it's true. Maybe Instagram is real for a lot of people, but I know it isn't for me, and it isn't for most of the influencers out there either. Why isn't it real? Because there aren't enough hours in the day and even reality TV shows aren't broadcast in real time.

Most influencers shoot content in bulk and use it over the course of a few months, or even years if they can pull it off. I don't wake up every morning and do my hair and makeup, choose the right outfit, and then pose somewhere in my house that is of course spotless and completely tidy at all times. I don't leave my house every day in a different outfit and head to a trendy spot downtown just to take a photo for that day's Instagram post. My life doesn't allow for that,

68

and even if it did, it's a really inefficient way of doing things. Are there influencers out there who do that? Yes, there are. Is that the case for the majority? Absolutely not.

The Truth About Bulk Content

If there's one thing an influencer always needs, it's new and fresh content to publish to feed the beast of social media. The truth about this content is that the vast majority of influencers out there, myself included, shoot a massive amount of content in the span of a few hours.

If you see that an influencer has a feed full of amazing outfits in urban settings, it's likely that she packed a pile of clothes, shoes, bags and accessories, threw them into the back of her car and drove around to different spots for an afternoon to shoot everything she would need to post for the foreseeable future.

I can't count the number of times I've changed outfits in the back of my husband's pickup truck while he adjusted light settings on the camera just so that we could take a series of photos all in one session. And boy, you haven't lived until you've changed into skinny jeans in the back of a car while six months pregnant. It isn't as exhilarating as it sounds, believe me.

I've also had the opportunity to do photoshoots in luxury show homes and that feels like a big treat, not just because the lighting is almost always amazing, but because you're able to do outfit changes in a bathroom or bedroom instead of within the confines of your car.

Is this luxury property my home? No. But I'm transparent about that when I tag the builder as a professional courtesy, citing the show home model name. "Your home is #goals" often shows up in the comment feed because no matter how many different houses I shoot content in, no one seems to know the difference, or at least they don't care to.

Posting In Real Time Isn't Always an Option

It's important to note that one of the main reasons that posting in real time doesn't work is because brands are asking to approve content days, weeks or months in advance of it going live. That's why you'll see a photo on an influencer's feed of her sitting in her living room with her family when you know she's *actually* on vacation in Mexico. Why is she talking about one thing in her sponsored stories, but you just saw her at the grocery store? Because that content was contractually scheduled to go live that day and was created as far back as a few months ago.

I'm not afraid to say that I've fudged reality on social media…but not in the way that you're thinking. I have never done anything like use a toilet seat over a backdrop to pretend I'm on an airplane. I've never "faked" it.

What I have done is "bend" reality a little bit. I don't do this to lie or to make my life seem like something it isn't. I've really just done this because content creation is time consuming AF and I've had to do a bit of recycling to keep up with demand. And yes, I did just say "recycling". That snowy photo I just posted? Yeah, it's from 2018 and it's now 2021 but my hair is the same and you don't remember that photo from three years ago, so no one is the wiser.

Want to know all of the ways that influencers "bend" reality on their feeds? Read on as I demystify the realities of Instagram!

Misconception: The Extended Foreign Trip

In 2018 my husband and I took a trip to Japan after which I posted photos on my social media for a few weeks. I did this partly because I had so many amazing photos to use and I wanted to share the incredible experiences that we had, but also because I needed some time to get my feet back under me to create new content after we returned from the trip (jetlag waits for no one!). I bumped into a neighbour who told me she couldn't believe we had been able to get away for so many weeks and I honestly laughed out loud at her confusion.

I told her that we were only there for about twelve days, and she replied with "But your Instagram…". I literally laughed at her and said: *"Instagram isn't real."*

Misconception: Her House is Always Picture Perfect

This is one of my favorite misconceptions because if you've ever watched my Instagram Stories, you'll see piles of things to be put away, toys scattered all over the floor and post-it notes listing things I need to do around the house covering my kitchen cabinetry. When you see a photo of me posed in a cute corner of my home, what you might not realize is that I literally moved all of the junk from that area of my home to behind the camera, or outside of the camera's field of view.

See an influencer post a photo that's really zoomed in? Consider what's outside the view finder. What are they hiding? Is this the only well-lit area they could find at that particular time of day?

Something else you might notice is that influencers will post similar photos of their home seemingly over and over and over again. That's partly because there are only so many ways you can photograph a bathroom or kitchen or mud room space. The other part of this is that I bet they staged their home once and shot all of that content over the course of a day or two – and these photos are reposted every few months, just when you forgot how great that mud room floor tile was!

Fresh home content often shows up when an influencer gets a new rug or piece of furniture. No one can refresh or restyle rooms in their home often enough for a continuous feed of new content…and who would want to?

Misconception: Her Hair & Makeup Is Always On Point. Every. Single. Day.

Are there influencers who get dolled up every single day of the week? There sure are. I know a few of them and I've read their captions and listened to their stories telling other women that if they don't get up before their children every morning and do their hair and makeup that they aren't "caring for themselves". Cool. You do you, babe.

I'm going to wash my hair and do my makeup on the days that I know I need to take photos for content. And I'm going to try to take as many of those photos on those days that I possibly can. The glam required for some of these Instagram posts is real and most of us don't have the glam-up time available to do this on the daily. The truth is most of these influencers do this as a side hustle and few of them are going to get this glammed up for their shift at the bank or a downtown office.

Misconception: She Looks Flawless and Full of Energy (And I Know She Was Pregnant Then!)

I feel like I need to come clean on this one. The first 16 weeks of each of my pregnancies were rough. I had such low blood pressure that I was basically bedridden for four months and looked really, really exhausted. In this time, I had contractual obligations to fulfill, and I had to appear in those photos. What did I do? Well, makeup can only do so much to hide those tired eyes and dark circles, so I used Photoshop to make myself look much more bright-eyed. And you know what? I have no regrets. I wasn't ready to tell the world I was pregnant yet, and I didn't want to answer questions about why I looked completely bagged, so I cheated a little.

This is another time in my life when I reused old photos for my Instagram feed because I felt too physically awful to shoot new content. There's no doubt that after I announced my pregnancies that some of my followers scrolled back in my feed and wondered how I looked so rested pre-announcement. Anyone in their first trimester who felt like garbage probably cursed those photos, too, thinking "Wow, what a B – that's not what being pregnant looks like" but I bet those girls didn't have a contractual obligation to post photos of themselves when they were keeping their baby bump a secret.

Misconception: She Just Had a Baby and She Looks Flawless

Many of the photos that I posted of myself postpartum (both times!) were actually of me before I was pregnant. This isn't because I wanted the world to think my body had bounced back to its pre-baby form, but it was really just out of exhaustion and the pure lack of time and energy it takes to get photoshoot ready while caring for a newborn child, or in my case, a 16-month old and a newborn at the same time.

I'm also not someone who posts many photos of myself in swimwear or workout clothes, so this made it a lot easier to get away with. I also delivered both of my children in the winter, so posting photos of myself in sweaters pre or post baby didn't really look all that different.

I bent the rules, but I wasn't unrealistic with it. I also posted a few pregnant and postpartum bikini photos for a swimsuit campaign – and those were entirely authentic, weren't edited or retouched, and were posted in real time. This was because I wanted women to feel comfortable in their bodies no matter what stage of life they were going through.

Misconception: She Had a Baby Yesterday and She's Already Out Shopping at a Store Event

This one is kind of twofold for me. Four days after the birth of my first baby I did attend a brand event at a big box store, and in a snowstorm no less. Everyone saw my announcement on Instagram that I'd had the baby and were convinced that I wouldn't show up to the event that morning. Was it crazy? Yes. But this was really just a casual shopping event and I didn't need to appear in any of the content.

Also, to know me is to know that I naturally have an incredible amount of energy, so doing something like this wasn't exactly outside of my wheelhouse. Besides, I was already up with the baby at the crack of dawn and awake anyways, so why not go out?

Fast-forward to the birth of my second little one. I had a contractual obligation to post a photo of me at a department store around my due date. Because I didn't know when I was going to go into labour, I took a few photos of myself holding large boxes in front of my baby belly that I could use post-delivery where I didn't look like I was 39 weeks pregnant (think: pregnant SJP as *Carrie Bradshaw* in *A Woman's Right to Shoes*[4]).

I ended up posting one of these photos after I delivered my baby and after I'd announced her arrival. Otherwise, I would have had to go down to the store 48 hours postpartum to shoot new content. And we all know that was *not* going to happen.

Misconception: Her Children Are Always Perfect and Well-Behaved

Photographing children of any age can be like herding cats. My kids are very busy little people so to get a photograph of them while they aren't moving is quite a challenge. Some influencers might have more docile children who easily comply with sitting still, but

---

[4] Reference: HBO's Sex and The City: Season 6, Episode 9

for most of us it's a rapid-fire of photos on your camera's sport mode to capture one, maybe two useable photos.

The truth is you don't know how many snaps it really took to get the photo that you see. The same goes for fur-children, especially outdoors. It's taken several attempts to get photos of us at the park with our dog who is heavily invested in chasing every squirrel she sees!

Misconception: She Works With So Many Amazing Brands

You see a post on Instagram in which an influencer has mentioned a brand by tagging them in the comments and you think to yourself: "Wow, how did she land a collaboration with them?!" Influencers tag brands in their posts all the time; it doesn't mean that they're working with a brand or that the post is sponsored in any way. The tag could be a professional courtesy, or it could be a way of trying to get a brand's attention to show them that you already wear or use their products.

Sometimes brands will repost a photo that they've been tagged in or feature the post on their stories, which can be great exposure for an influencer. If someone thinks it's sponsored and it elevates the influencer's status, then bonus, but it's not the reality.

Confession: I've Recycled Old Content on Instagram

I've reused content on my Instagram feed, and this is something most influencers do on a regular basis. If you're an influencer who has never posted the same photo twice or posted yourself in the same outfit twice but from slightly different angles from the same shoot, then good for you. I wish I had that kind of time. Here are a few more ways that I've recycled content on my Instagram feed:

Let's say I did a photoshoot for a parka, but I took photos of myself posing in a few different ways. I can spread these photos out over the course of a few months (seasonally, of course) with captions that talk about all sorts of things either related or completely unrelated to the photo itself. I can also use these parka photos for the next few winters, provided I don't change a ton about my appearance (i.e. going from blonde to brunette, etc.).

Some of the photos that I posted of myself when I was pregnant with my second child were from my first pregnancy. I only have so much bandwidth and patience to pose for photos, so rather than shoot a ton of new content every time I needed it, I just used a few photos from the first time around. I mean, I was still pregnant, so I wasn't *lying* per se, it was just a different child in utero in the photo.

I've recycled holiday content from year to year, too. Let's be honest: there are only so many ways to decorate a table for Thanksgiving, Easter, and Christmas and I bet you can't remember what I shared for inspo last year let alone two, three, five or more years ago. I'll re-style my table and post about it when I get a new set of dishes or a table runner that I'm obsessed with.

Instagram Versus Reality: What's Going on Behind the Scenes

I think it's important to note that influencers don't always fake content because they're fake people, but because they're actually *real* people. You often only know a fraction of a fraction of a fraction of what's going on in an influencer's life. Not every influencer is an over-sharer and many choose to keep certain parts of their lives private. Consider my example of reposting old photos of myself while I was in the early stages of each of my pregnancies. I wasn't ready to share that I was pregnant yet, and rather than pull myself out of bed and try to take photos while suppressing nausea, I just used old photos.

Maybe that influencer that you follow had to post this week to maintain their momentum in the app's algorithm, but they just lost a grandparent or a friend, or are going through a rough breakup. Maybe they have terrible period cramps or food poisoning or just had surgery and they don't want to divulge these personal details to their audience.

Some things are faked because influencers themselves are empty and fake. Some things are faked because life itself is very real and messy.

CHAPTER 9

INFLUENCER FOMO
(THE FEAR OF MISSING OUT)

It's no secret that social media can make many of us feel like we're not enough. You see an influencer post something to their Instagram feed and you immediately feel less-than. You wonder how does she do it all? How is her house so clean and tidy and her kids are so well-behaved, and her blowout and makeup are flawless as can be? Her house looks like it's out of a magazine and my house looks like trash. She and her husband are so in love, and everything is perfect, and they go on fancy dates and are clearly having sex all the time, because look at the pics she's posting, and have you *read* her captions?!

It's easy to tell an influencer to "stay in their own lane" and not worry about what those around them are doing, but on the flip side, influencers need to keep up with content trends so they can't operate with blinders on, either. To be an influencer requires an incredibly thick skin and that's not always easy. Often influencers get so caught up in what their peers are doing that they lose sight of their "why", their brand identity and even their own sense of self, or worse, their self-esteem.

The Cognitive Dissonance is Real

Here's something you might not realize about influencers: even though they know the game of Instagram better than anyone else, when they see another influencer's post, they feel all the same disappointment about their lives...and then some. The cognitive dissonance is *very* real. For example: an influencer is scrolling through Instagram and they see that several of their peers are on a sponsored weekend getaway with a travel company. A non-influencer may see these posts and feel disappointed that their life isn't full of exciting weekend getaways, whereas a fellow-influencer will see these posts and feel that same disappointment topped with feelings of "Why wasn't I invited? I create great travel content! I feel so left out and rejected."

Further to this: a non-influencer may think that these are really beautiful vacation photos or that it's nice that these people have friends to travel with. An influencer will wonder how these people look so flawless in their photos, how they got just the right lighting and also feel like they were left out of a "girl's trip".

This is interesting because it's likely that the influencer knows what it takes to get those photos *and* what early hour you would have to wake up at to capture them. It's also interesting that the influencer will feel left out of an experience they think is something that it truly isn't. This is likely a group of girls that are not friends. They may or may not be friendly colleagues either. They will be waiting their turn or jostling for the perfect shots for their social feeds, not bonding in pjs over glasses of bubbly.

The left-out influencer is also wondering how these other influencers had the time to take this fun trip, not remembering that these trips are seldom fun, they're *work* trips. They are a quick in-and-out to take whatever content is required with very little, if any, downtime.

"But how *does* she do it all?" Some influencers like to keep their trade secrets just that – a secret. They love being able to appear as if they are a superior superwoman, able to do it all with a perfect blow out and spotless home. They don't share that they have a nanny, cleaning service, meal deliveries and likely an executive assistant or even a full team working for them behind the scenes. Meanwhile, other influencers embrace the chaos of their lives as a part of their brand, yet somehow other influencers don't believe that either. Shrug.

Influencer FOMO Reactions

There are a few types of influencer reactions to their own personal FOMO when they see another influencer getting something they think they should be getting. What I'm hoping to convey here is just how competitive the industry can be and that influencers are real people, too, who experience feelings of disappointment, envy, and sometimes motivation.

The Why Not _ME_? Influencer Reaction

It's natural that an immediate reaction to seeing an influencer posting in collaboration with a brand you love is to wonder "why not me?" This is no different than anyone seeing their friend's new home, new car, fancy vacation, new (insert anything here) and comparing their own lives – it just happens on a more frequent basis in the influencer world because so many products are sent their way.

The "_Why_ _NOT_ Me?" Influencer Reaction

In contrast to feeling downtrodden and like brands don't love you, an influencer might see another influencer's post and think to themselves "why _not_ me?" because clearly that post was a signal that a brand they love must work with influencers. Some influencers will turn their observations of their peers into motivation to go after those same brands.

83

This can go either way, though, as a brand may have already used up their marketing budget in the campaign they just saw online or they could be thrilled to learn that other influencers want to work with them, too. In the influencer space, however, others may view them as chasing or copycatting their peers' collaborations.

The "She Has It Therefore I Must Have It" Influencer Reaction

Some influencers only want what other influencers have because other influencers have it – not because they *actually* want or need it themselves. If another influencer has the latest and greatest (anything) product, then she must have it too, either in order not to be outdone or some other competitive reasoning.

For some it is a feeling of equality that if an influencer that they hold in high esteem received the same product collaboration, then they too, must be equal to that esteem. For others it is a sense of entitlement that if a product is out there and up for grabs that they should be gifted it because of their follower count or content quality.

The "Influenced" Influencer Reaction

Even influencers struggle to determine if another influencer is genuine in their sales pitch to their audience. They see a sponsored post and start wondering if they buy that product, will their life be better? Does this influencer like this product? It seems like a weird fit that she's pushing this product, but if she's trying to get me to buy it, then she must love it, too, right? The term "cognitive dissonance" bears repeating.

The "IDGAF" Influencer Reaction

The influencer who doesn't care about what other influencers are doing is either a total badass or a myth. It's easy to compare yourself to others in general, and natural to compare yourself to your colleagues, even if only sometimes. But these influencers do exist. They stay in their own lane and when you meet them in person, they exude a certain level of cool confidence and decorum that is unmatched by their peers. They know themselves; they know their brand and they know their message and they stay true to that. They may choose to engage with their peers online, but only because their peers are fans and audience members.

This is the standard I try to hold myself to, but it's hard not to fall into the trap of wondering why I wasn't sent an invite for an event or perhaps why a colleague in another niche earned a collaboration with a brand I've been dying to work with.

After all, I'm human, too.

CHAPTER 10

THE "MOM BLOGGER" SHAMING IS REAL

If you think mom-shaming is harsh in real life, trying being an influencer with children. Online bullying, hate mail and trolls are all very real things that influencers deal with on the regular and it's that much worse for those in the "mom blogger" space. Are there people who would walk up to a mom at the grocery store and make scathing comments about her children and their clothing/behavior/appearance/state of being? There sure are, but those incidents are a lot more rare than the online trolls who seek out influencers on a daily basis and make rude comments just to be jerks.

Her Children Are Reluctant Props

Mom bloggers seem to face more online hate than any other category of influencers and that could be because they are among the most popular with brands for paid collaborations. Mom bloggers are so frequently used by brands for paid placements for countless reasons. Moms are trusted. Moms are approachable and viewed as more real and authentic. Moms are often a home's primary purchaser. Moms are competitive and everyone wants to have what the "it mom" is using for her kids – and brands know that. Moms wield a lot of influence which is great for advertising, but the other side of that is very unkind.

Beyond the level of regular negativity an influencer can experience for her appearance, personality, online persona, life choices, etc., mom bloggers are criticized for their parenting, their lack of parenting, their health and vaccination choices, their posed or candid photos, what their kids wear/say/do/eat, if they are potty trained or not, if you called it potty training or not, if they appear to be too eager in front of the camera or resistant entirely.

These women are accused of using their children as props to get free stuff, or as pawns for more paid campaigns. A mom blogger is criticized for featuring her children too often (exploitation) or not often enough (inauthentic, neglectful).

I think it's important to note that not all children are unwilling participants. There are kids who love the fame and attention – and these kids love all the extra toys, trips and experiences that this business brings to their family, too. I've had people ask me things like "She's always putting her daughter in her photos and on her stories and it feels like it's against her will." My honest response is "Have you met her daughter? This kid lives for it."

Some kids love being filmed and being in photos. Granted, they can't completely conceptualize that images and videos of them being posted to social media carries certain implications, but that's because they're children. What I'm getting at here is that not every child is a forced prop in their influencer parent's photos, and it should be up to the parent to determine the level of risk they are taking on by displaying their children online with whatever frequency they choose.

My Experience With Internet Trolls

I honestly don't get much hate, if any, online. I think my audience knows that I'm a pretty straight shooter and I make it a known part of my brand that what I share is well-researched (i.e. I don't talk out of my ass). I don't share anything incredibly polarizing and I don't share my personal decisions that could cause people to share their very... determined opinions, shall we say? I did have one experience that I think is worth mentioning.

When I was pregnant with my first little one I met another local influencer for coffee. Much of her brand was in the "mommy blogger" space and one of the only things I remember from our meeting was her telling me to prepare myself for trolls and hate mail now that I was pregnant, and the public knew it. Honestly, she wasn't wrong. It only took a moment for what a few internet trolls considered a huge misstep.

A few days later, I posted a photo on my feed where I was holding a bottle of pink bubbles.

My caption read:

"This is me mixing patterns! I'm not usually one to be bold with what I wear but I couldn't resist pairing this polka dot apron with this striped @bananarepublicfactory bell-sleeved dress! I maintained the same colour palette so things didn't get too crazy.

P.S. Just because I'm not drinking *doesn't mean I can't serve these wonderful pink bubbles to my guests!"*

Most of the comments I received on the post and in my DMs were along the lines of "I bet you're saving that for when you pop!" or "Glad you're still sharing recommendations!" or "Cute apron!".

I did receive one quite nasty direct message that started off with "I only followed you so that I could send you this message". *Great, so this person doesn't even know me or follow me at all.*

She went on to tell me that although this was none of her business, she felt the need to tell me how appalled she was by my post. Because I had just announced that I was pregnant, she felt it was incredibly important that she tell me that drinking while pregnant was incredibly harmful to my unborn child. And that although it was, again, none of her business, she thought I should be smart enough to know that and because I clearly wasn't, I should not be "influencing" anyone.

Should I have posted this? In hindsight, maybe not. After all, I was pregnant, but I figured the disclaimer would make it okay. The bottle was sealed. I wasn't drinking it. I didn't drink it. I clearly stated that I wasn't drinking it. I also took the photo several weeks before I knew I was pregnant and thus did not have a visible baby bump. I was not encouraging pregnant women to consume alcohol.

But that didn't matter because some people just don't read captions.

The Overshare Opens You Up to Ridicule

I personally don't talk about parenting on my blog or social media because it isn't on brand for me. I'm a blogger and I'm a mom. I'm not a "mom blogger" and I've been careful to purposefully avoid this space. If I share anything parenting related, it's the stroller that I love that makes my life easier. I don't share parenting tips, potty training progress and methods, sleep training or lack thereof, or the personal health information of my children.

To be honest, this comes from me being a fairly private person, but also because I want to keep my blog focused and uncluttered.

Furthermore, I don't want to open myself up to these kinds of discussions or the ridicule and online shaming that may subsequently occur.

There are "mom bloggers" who share every image of their child's life from breastfeeding to baby-led-weaning, potty training to vaccine appointments. They have chosen to raise their children in the fishbowl of their Instagram feed without realizing or even considering the long-term implications.

In the short term, the sharing of this information is viewed by the public as an invitation for commentary and sharing of their opinions. After all, don't influencers need and want more comments on their posts? Negative comments are still comments, aren't they? Ah, the double-edged sword strikes again.

The Golden Rule is Gone

I think we all remember learning as children that if you don't have something nice to say, it's best not to say anything at all. This is clearly not the case when it comes to internet trolls who feel their anonymity protects them. If an influencer receives too much hate and negativity from a certain account, they will block or report them to Instagram, but sometimes that isn't enough. Some of these people will create new accounts just to send nasty messages to influencers that they despise.

To be honest, it must be nice to have that kind of free time that you can create multiple Instagram accounts, seek out influencers and then send them scathing messages every time you believe they misstep.

CHAPTER 11

THE INFAMOUS BLACK SQUARE

In June of 2020 the Black Lives Matter movement gained prominence in the wake of several high-profile police-related deaths of African American people in the United States. This was an incredibly important movement that brought discussions to the forefront that were long overdue. I'm not here to talk about the significance of the movement or its importance, but instead how this changed the influencer landscape. Many influencers chose to post (or not post) a black square to their Instagram feed, and this is an anecdotal snapshot of the mayhem that ensued.

Muted and Listening

The BLM movement reinforced a long-held belief of mine that when it comes to social causes, influencers are in a lose-lose situation. Say too much, and an influencer isn't allowing the right voices to be heard. Say too little, and an influencer is not using their platform for such an incredibly important cause. Say anything at all, and an influencer is accused of saying too much, saying the wrong thing, being insensitive, being ignorant and of course the grand prize of all, being called a racist.

If an influencer didn't post that they were "muted and listening" because maybe they were *actually* muted and listening, then the angry masses would go after them for not "doing their part for the movement". This must mean that if it wasn't posted on social media then it didn't happen, or an influencer isn't thinking about it? Who can tell?

To show just how inclusive they were, influencers began sharing the profiles of the "influencers of colour" in their networks. If they had children, they would share lists of books about race, diversity, and inclusion, and how to have an "anti-racist baby" *(seriously, this is a thing)*.

Some viewed this as a celebration of racial diversity whereas others saw it as opportunistic tokenization. Influencers were told they should do *something*, but what that *something* was still remains incredibly unclear. Rather than focusing the attention on the movement itself, the internet trolls went on a veritable witch hunt to seek out those influencers that they deemed weren't doing enough for the movement, whose feeds lacked diversity, who said too much, who didn't say enough, who didn't know what to say or really anything else you can think of in-between.

Emotions were running incredibly high during this time and some situations were completely devoid of logic and reason. Some influencers were "cancelled" without the opportunity to defend themselves because any unintentional wrongdoing, real or perceived, was somehow unforgiveable. In contrast, other influencers used this as an opportunity to rise to the top of their field with newfound popularity.

A Racial Justice Movement for Some = Opportunity for Others

An influencer that I used to follow who is a self-described woman of colour, but very notably not black or First Nations, felt that the BLM movement offered the perfect opportunity to elevate her brand. She took to her Instagram stories where she noted that before this movement, she *felt* that she had been rejected by brands based on her race, without providing any evidence to support this.

She stated that now these brands were seeing the value in working with influencers who are "women of colour" and recognized that this would help them reach new audiences. My immediate reaction was that I was disappointed that brands would reject an influencer based on this criteria in the first place, but it's great that they are now working with influencers based on merit.

Here's where she lost me: She continued to say that she would be working with a number of high-profile brands (*good for her!*) **but** that "all you white influencers need to make space and not be mad when women of colour start taking work away from you". *Um, what now?* I'm pretty sure "make space" means that there is room for all of us as *equals*, not "there is no longer room for anyone who is white".

I'm pretty sure equality does not mean displacing someone based on race. I'm more than happy to make space, but let's share that space and earn work in a meritocracy, and if not based solely on merit, then based on long-standing business relationships and networking skills.

Not only did she hijack a movement that had nothing to do with her, but she also then proceeded to misuse the expression "make space". To "make space" does not mean to "displace" as she so incorrectly stated. Unfortunately for those who weren't entirely wise to this new "woke" term, this only caused anger, anxiety, and further division.

Was she effectively taking work away from BIPOC[5] and non-BIPOC influencers alike? Maybe there were some actual "women of colour" that could have received some of these campaigns to elevate their profile and show some real diversity in advertising.

---

[5] BIPOC: acronym for Black, Indigenous, and People of Colour

I'm going to assume that she doesn't care how she gets work or if she displaces anyone to do so, just as long as she "gets hers".

There are a few influencer campaigns where you can say that an influencer's race or culture are the reason a brand would choose one qualified influencer over another. Examples that come to mind are campaigns for holidays such as Hanukkah, Diwali, or Lunar New Year. But race has nothing to do with your ability to market laundry soap.

I believe in diverse representation in marketing, but I feel uncomfortable when there are influencers who are beginning to sell their race and the fact that they are non-white as a part of their personal brand. In turn, they are bragging to other influencers about their success in playing this card and encouraging them to do the same. It's a dangerous precedent and this kind of behavior should not be encouraged, in my opinion.

My Experience with a Troll During BLM

If you know me, you know that I do *not* virtue signal – ever. It goes against every fiber of my being so keep that in mind while you read this.

I posted the black square to my Instagram feed.

I didn't post it because everyone else posted it, but rather to show my friends of colour that I stood by them in solidarity and that their feelings were important to me. I didn't tokenize any of my friends or colleagues on my Instagram stories or even mention that I had been a brand ambassador for a Black-owned haircare brand for two years prior to this movement taking hold (which I was). I didn't feel the need to show my anti-racist bona fides because I believe that people should be judged on their actions.

A white woman in her early twenties who I have never met and has never followed me on Instagram or read a single one of my blog posts, sent me a direct message accusing me of being racist for patronizing a favorite local business of mine. She believed that their staff was not "diverse enough" and my patronage was only adding to the problem. I want to note here that this business employs a staff that is a visual cultural mosaic and was half-owned by a "person of colour", so when I informed her thusly, she proceeded to attack me and tell me to "educate myself", whatever that means in this context.

Accusation #1: "You're not doing enough for the movement."

Of course, my immediate reaction was "You have no idea what I am or am not doing for *any* movement, including this one" and I meant that. What the trolls (including this one) might not realize is that some of the influencers that they were sending hate mail to do a lot of quiet work to support women and communities of colour all around the world.

Just because they don't broadcast it on their social media does not mean the work isn't being done. In fact, much of the important and meaningful work being done in our communities isn't shown on social media because it's just that – *meaningful*. Those doing the important work are too busy doing that important work to stop to share it on Instagram. And they aren't doing it for the recognition of their service on social media either.

Accusation #2: "Your feed lacks diversity."

This is very true, and I'm quite fine with it. My Instagram feed does lack racial diversity. In case you don't follow me on Instagram, let me give you the gist of what you'll see if you took a quick scroll through my feed: Photos of me, photos of my home or other inspiring interior design concepts, photos of me, photos of wine, food, or travel destinations, photos of me, photos of products that I love, photos of me and the occasional photo of my husband or children all mixed within more (wait for it!) photos of me.

I don't post photos of my friends or extended family so there's no way of knowing if they are a homogenous group or not. From my Instagram feed, you could assume that I have no friends at all, because they aren't featured. I did have a friend who is a "woman of colour" make a joke that she should come to my house and pose for photos in my newly renovated pantry to help me "diversify". But seriously: is this the requirement now?

#EducateYourself and Your Audience

I cannot speak to the experience of a black person in America, but I can speak about how any of us can create meaningful change in the justice system. When the case of Breonna Taylor hit the news, I took a different approach than other influencers.

Rather than the empty gesture of posting #JusticeForBreonna to my social media, I sought to educate my audience on what happened in that case and how they could make meaningful change going forward. It's important to note here that I live in Canada and am not an American citizen so I can only push for change in Canada.

I did my research and learned that "No-Knock Warrants" (the catalyst to this tragedy) were often granted in Canada. I informed my audience of this and told them that if they were against this practice that they should contact their Member of Parliament (US Equivalent = Member of Congress) and our federal Justice Minister expressing their desire to see these laws changed.

I even included the email address of the Justice Minister at the time. I wanted to offer my audience a tangible action for helping create meaningful change that wasn't reposting hashtags or shouting into the abyss of the internet.

I believed that by educating myself on the heart of an important social issue and sharing my findings with my audience that I was doing my part. I still believe this. I also didn't share the information just for the sake of it, either. I included a call-to-action that was simple for my audience to do, and that could *actually* affect change.

I do the same thing every election cycle by encouraging my audience to research the platforms of every political party and then vote based on their personal beliefs. I continuously encourage my audience to reach out to their representatives at various levels of government to have their voices heard on the issues that matter to them in their communities.

I don't expect all influencers to do this, and if they aren't educated on the issues or our political processes then I strongly recommend that they don't! Getting involved in the process in a meaningful way is something that I am passionate about and so I use my platform carefully to do so, when appropriate.

CHAPTER 12

HASHTAGS DON'T SAVE LIVES

The many, many news events of 2020-2021 exposed a lot about our society and perhaps even more so in the influencer space. Influencers taking to their platforms to try and impact social change on a large scale should have been a wonderful thing, but instead, it exposed how vapid and empty so many of them truly are. It showed us how very little influencers *actually* do to create change in their communities, both local and global, and how they believe that hashtags are the most impactful tool in their belt.

Hashtags don't save lives. But what does that statement even mean? In today's society it seems that a post to social media with the hashtag du-jour counts as "doing something". As the world continues to virtue signal as a temporary solution to solving its problems, influencers play their part and encourage this kind of intentional inaction on a regular basis. To be fair, posting a photo with a hashtag is far less effort than taking any real action in helping those who need it most. At the end of the day, it is just one more "awareness" campaign that we don't need.

Influencers Need to #EducateThemselves

The more I watched influencers try to tackle the social issues of the day, the more it became apparent how entirely ignorant they were on these issues and even more so on the greater scale of disputes going on in the world. No one looks to an influencer and expects a Rhodes Scholar, but if someone is going to go online and share information with a large audience, there should be some responsibility to getting the facts straight.

I'm not going to dive into the issues and their specifics, but rather share what I observed about influencers trying to use their platforms to talk about these social issues while falling so startlingly short.

The #FreeGaza Conflict

The Arab-Israeli conflict is perhaps the most long-running conflict our world has ever known. It's fair to say that it is not even a centuries-old conflict but rather one that is millennia-old and so full of nuance and detail that it is impossible to discuss in a mere social media post, let alone here. There are countless sides to this particular conflict, none of which I am going to get into, especially because this is a book about influencers.

The side I'm taking on this issue is that most influencers are ignorant and are really just astonishingly fucking stupid. I've never considered the majority of influencers to be the brightest on the block, but on this particular issue, their ignorance hit new levels that surprised even me. I watched as countless influencers posted/reposted statements of misinformation on the conflict to their social media feeds, all under the guise that this conflict was somehow shocking and brand new to the news cycle.

I watched groups of vapid airheads post photos of themselves in bikinis or selfies at raw juice bars with the hashtag #FreeGaza. The cognitive dissonance of that in itself was hard to watch. I read nonsensical captions, heard incredibly ignorant conspiracy theories (i.e. Hamas is funded by Israel) and watched pointless Instagram stories full of statements of how much they "can't believe what's happening over there". Really? *REALLY?!* You can't believe that there is a conflict happening in that particular region of the world? Were you literally born yesterday?

I can't decide if this is an indictment on our education system that these influencers have no concept of world events over the last five years, let alone any of the context of what's occurred in this region throughout the twentieth century and for centuries before that. I want to blame education, but on the other hand, Wikipedia is free and readily available to us all, so is there really an excuse?

You Have a Platform, Therefore You Need to Use It

"You have a platform, therefore you need to use it for XYZ cause." If an influencer shared an opinion on every cause, news story, charity, war or act of genocide, or non-profit organization trying to gain awareness and support, they wouldn't have any space on their Instagram feeds to talk about anything else, let alone to sell you anything to pay their own bills. There is tremendous pressure put on influencers to use their platform for a good cause, but it's also a double-edged sword.

Most influencers don't have the knowledge of world issues and current events, or really the required intelligence, to navigate this correctly. On one hand they're guilty of hastily sharing misinformation, in large part out of ignorance on the issues. But on the other hand, this hasty posting is because if they don't post quickly enough after a news story breaks, they could get cancelled for not caring about the world around them.

What's an influencer to do? Do they only post about the issues that they care about and leave the rest behind? Do they just stick to peddling their product of the day and act as if unaware of what's happening in their own backyards?

For those who demonize influencers for not diving into the news, consider if you would rather someone with 50,000 or 100,000 or more followers on social media getting their "facts" from someone who is unclear on the facts themselves, just so they can appear "aware". Pressuring influencers to discuss topics that they are unfamiliar with doesn't encourage them to educate themselves on an issue, but rather contributes to the continuous spread of misinformation and blurring of facts.

Influencers are for the most part, all about the quick post that is required of them, not about learning the nuance and facts about an issue to educate their audiences. If influencers could just stick to what they *actually* know instead of being forced to share whatever trending cause or political hashtag is deemed important right now, society might be a little better off. Or at least a little less angry and ignorant.

Because after all, hashtags don't save lives.

CHAPTER 13

THE ENGAGEMENT GAME

More likes on social media posts are all anyone *really* wants or cares about, right?! In all reality it's followers, likes, saves, comments, shares, mentions, and tags. You know, all the things that *actually* matter in life (I say, sarcastically).

Keeping up with engagement is a full-time job for influencers. They must like posts to get likes on their posts, leave comments to get comments, follow others to get followers, know which songs are trending so their Reels get more views, research hashtags and know how many of those are deemed the *right* ones to use so their posts have further reach and of course, trying to beat the myth/reality of the ever-changing algorithm.

If you're reading this and thinking that somehow Engagement = Self-Esteem or Higher Self-Worth, this isn't real life, this is the business of an Instagram influencer. I'm sure there are influencers that care how well their posts do because it translates into their version of love and acceptance, but I'm not going down that rabbit hole. Here Engagement = Popularity that translates into a monetary worth to brands so that you can get paid collaborations, and lots more of them.

Why Engagement Matters

Getting engagement on social media, particularly Instagram, is hard.

You can ask all the questions you want in your captions to try and engage your audience, but the truth is, some people just like to scroll through the photos, watch a few videos, maybe read a caption or two and then carry on with their *real* lives. You'd think that likes would have increased on content when Instagram created the 'double tap' feature to like a photo, but even that can be too much effort for some.

Most users scrolling through Instagram, see a photo and think to themselves "that's nice", and move on. That sounds great in theory, but they didn't *actually engage* with your content so they're effectively worthless to an influencer. Maybe instead of commenting on the post publicly, that person sends the influencer a direct message with questions and comments. Those are lovely messages to receive, and it's likely very meaningful to engage with a member of your audience, but that conversation doesn't show up in the vanity metrics.

The cold hard truth is that those particular metrics are what influencers rely on to make a living and survive.

Engagement in the form of likes and comments, and now saves and shares, count towards this score. These are important to brands because it's a metric that they can use to determine whether they want to work with an influencer, and then gauge the success of a paid collaboration with them after the fact. But getting this kind of engagement on post after post can be hard to come by – and many will blame the ever-changing algorithm for that. I personally believe it could be any number of factors, but the algorithm certainly doesn't help.

I'm not so self-involved to believe that everyone in my audience should love and comment on absolutely everything that I create or post or say. No influencer (or account) can have an entire audience full of adoring fans who like and comment on every single piece of content they have ever posted or will post. It's just not the reality that we live in.

The Engagement Game

So just how do influencers get such great engagement on their posts? Every influencer has some amount of authentic engagement from their audience, but to maintain or stimulate additional engagement for their own content, influencers need to engage on other accounts' posts. This comes back to my earlier statements on these being *social* networks. But how do you find other willing participants? Enter the "engagement pod".

For those of you not familiar with the term, an "engagement pod" is basically when a group of influencers or social media personalities create a chat group either in Instagram Direct Messages, WhatsApp, Telegram or some other chat platform. Every time they post, they notify the group that they have new content so that everyone can engage with their post.

In return they're supposed to go back and like, comment, and save all of the most recent posts of the other accounts in the pod. Remember when I talked about the unspoken social contract of reciprocal engagement? Pods strictly enforce that contract with their members. Skip engaging on a few posts and that pod will kick you out.

Do I participate in engagement pods? Yes, I do. Why? In all honesty, I'm an incredibly busy human being with countless things on the go at any given moment of the day. I can't remember all of the people that I want to make sure that I comment on their content when they post - because I genuinely do love their content and want to support them. I also don't have endless time to scroll and see what everyone I follow is up to on a regular enough basis, so for a few key creators that I love and want to support, this is the best way for me to do that. The algorithm also doesn't always feed me the content that I want to see the most so these groups serve as a 'to do list' of whose content I want to see when I'm using the app.

Pods also serve as online forums for those of us in the same industry. We can ask each other questions, offer support, troubleshoot and even celebrate one another. I'll never forget a message I read in one of my pods while I was pregnant with my first daughter and several days overdue. It said: "You better post in this group the second you have that baby because all of her Instagram Aunties can't wait to meet her!"

There is a lot of criticism of influencers commenting on other influencer's content all the time. But these are our colleagues and peers, and this is the main platform that we use to communicate with one another, so there shouldn't be much surprise if we comment on each other's posts.

Engagement Is a Full Time Job

A fellow influencer once told me that pods will never provide the kind of engagement required to be successful in this business long term. She discouraged me in seeking out a new pod of like-minded creators with content that I genuinely loved because she felt the engagement would not be authentic.

She mentioned that building meaningful relationships with other accounts was what really mattered for lasting engagement – but in the same breath she mentioned that she outsourced much of her commenting and comment replies on her own account.

It was curious why an influencer who is known to participate in large pods to boost her own engagement numbers for likes and comments would be so adamant that this method of "drumming up engagement" on posts would fall flat and only serve me in the short term. Perhaps she thinks she is protecting her own business practices or maybe she was too embarrassed to mention that she found pods to be just as unavoidable as most of us do.

Before you judge her too harshly here, understand just how much time it requires to reply to 100+ comments on your own posts (in an engaging way), coupled with engaging on enough accounts to get them to engage with your posts regularly.

And remember that this is something influencers must do on a daily basis, or however often they post.

CHAPTER 14

BOOSTS, BOTS AND BUYING ENGAGEMENT

While increasing engagement should be on every influencer's mind, simply maintaining it is a full-time job. And ensuring that a post an influencer was paid to share receives the engagement a brand was counting on can cause significant anxiety. Poor engagement on sponsored posts can reflect badly on an influencer, even if it is completely out of their control. So if a post is performing inadequately, what's an influencer to do?

Asking For Engagement = Internet Panhandling

The newest trend on Instagram is influencers posting to their stories asking for "love" in the form of engagement on their most recent sponsored posts. I've seen two approaches to this: tugging on heartstrings with mild honesty and using incentives. Influencers will post to their stories thanking their audiences for their support while asking for more engagement going forward with statements like:

Like/comment/save/share so that it looks good to the brand so I can get more paid work.

This is how I feed my family/pay my bills/buy things for my babies.

Without your support, I couldn't do this.

Without your support, I wouldn't have taken this free trip to Mexico/Enjoyed this free dinner/insert whatever here.

How does an influencer's audience see this request for engagement? Probably something like this:

"Please, engage with my content so I can get paid to try to sell you more shit you don't need that I probably don't even like and have probably sold or donated by now."

Everyone knows that influencers are paid for their collaborations and not just because the FTC (the U.S. Federal Trade Commission) put disclosure guidelines in place (**HINT:** this is why you now see #AD #SPONSORED #GIFTED on posts).

Some influencers have even taken it so far as to post a warning on their stories on a Sunday night to notify their audience that a week full of advertising posts is coming up, *but* for everyone who engages on those sponsored posts, there will be a draw at the end of the week for a coffee gift card.

Is this an acceptable incentive? Is it bribery? Is it entirely inauthentic? Is it doing what they need to survive? Brands have caught on to this and have started adding clauses in their agreements that prohibit begging their audience for engagement on posts related to their paid campaign.

Brands Now Want to Boost Posts

There's a theory that the use of #AD and #SPONSORED tags to disclose when an influencer has been paid to promote a product has offered Instagram an internal "flag" of sorts. The theory, or myth, suggests that Instagram internally suppresses the engagement of posts that use these hashtags so that an influencer will have to pay the platform a fee to boost or promote the post for better engagement and visibility.

Why? It's likely because Instagram saw that influencers are using their platform to make money (and a lot of it!) and they wanted their piece of the pie. Instagram doesn't see any commission from the sponsored posts that brands pay influencers to create and post for them.

Influencer collaborations are effectively like selling the ad space on a billboard without owning the billboard – and the billboard owner doesn't see a dime.

But is the suppression of influencers' sponsored content a reality? Well, there might be some truth to this theoretical myth because now brands are including a boosting budget in their paid collaborations with influencers.

What does this mean? In a contract with an influencer, it will state that the brand will pay the influencer $1,500 for their post, but $500 of that must be used to "boost" the post to a certain selected group of ad viewers. Influencers are then required to submit the receipt from Facebook (the owners of Instagram) along with the demographic reach results of the boost for reimbursement.

Engagement Can Be Bought

Anything can be bought, including engagement. In the many discussions in this book about Instagram not being real, this is just one more reality that requires mentioning.

Don't believe me? A quick online search will bring up countless services that offer likes, views, impressions, comments, saves, shares, or any other engagement statistic an Instagram (or any other social platform) that anyone would need to augment for any purpose. But can't users *tell* that this engagement is inauthentic? Not always. Or maybe they don't have any idea that it isn't real. Even if they do, they might not care.

Ask yourself this honest question: Do you care if an account that you follow has thousands of likes per post if you love their content? Do you like them simply because they have a lot of engagement or because you *actually* like them?

Buying engagement is a careful balance, too, because an influencer's "engagement rate" must fall within a certain threshold. This "rate" is simply calculated by the total number of average likes and comments on a post divided by the total number of followers an influencer has. Too little overall engagement (likes and comments) and an influencer appears unpopular, or their large follower count may appear suspicious.

Too much engagement or too many likes and it looks inauthentic or shows a spike in an influencer's statistics. Too many likes but not enough comments and engagement will look like it was purchased. Basically, if an influencer has a certain number of followers, their posts should receive a certain amount of likes and comments.

Purchased engagement doesn't always come in the form of bots. Influencers can pay for premium spots in engagement pods where all the members of a pod must comment on their posts, but because they've paid for a "spot" they don't have to take the time to comment on anyone else's posts. The comments appear to be more genuine, and they are coming from real accounts and real users. The only difference here is the influencer paid for the convenience of not reciprocating with engagement.

Some PR firms and influencer agencies will claim to use software that determines if the followers and engagement that an influencer has are authentic. This sounds like a foolproof method until you learn that "bot farms"[6] are one step ahead of them.

Most of the "likes" that accounts purchase for their accounts come from other real accounts that are created by an unknown number of automated scripts controlled by Asian or Eastern European syndicates.

These are the different tools that are available to every user on Instagram, if you're willing to pay for them.

---

[6] "Bot Farm" refers to a collection of internet servers that simulate real users

CHAPTER 15

CHASING LIKES

It's hard to know if anything is authentic anymore. The content that influencers post to Instagram isn't entirely real. The timelines they post their content within aren't entirely real. The comments they receive on their posts aren't entirely real. The personal details they share about their lives are curated or completely manufactured to boost engagement. They endorse products that they don't use, like or care about.

The hustle is real, and the work ethic is definitely there, but that doesn't mean that the work itself is always meaningful.

No matter how much you get paid, how many comped vacations you get to take, how many gift boxes arrive at your front door, or how much celebrity you think you have, deep inside you have to know that nothing is real, you can't do this forever and there is always another influencer ready and willing to take your place.

Life is Content

Many influencers are now beginning to share every personal moment and milestone, good, bad or otherwise, to their social media. We're now seeing them invite professional photographers to document intimate life moments for the express purpose of sharing them online. And I'm not talking about engagements or weddings or birth announcements. I'm talking about labor, childbirth, stillbirth, and miscarriage – all while in hospital. The final moments of a child's life, the passing of a family member, or the euthanasia of a family pet. The more raw and intimate, seemingly the better.

Everything an influencer does in life is a content opportunity, but also in contrast, an obligation as well. It's a 24/7 gig that doesn't allow for breaks and isn't easy to walk away from. If you're daring enough to take a few weeks off (because maybe you had a baby or something), you'll spend weeks trying to rebuild the drop in vanity metrics and engagement.

I would love to do my hair and makeup "just because" - not because I need to take photos or feel the need to take photos because *hey, my hair and makeup are done today*. I would love to enter a hotel room and collapse on the bed and relax or even unpack before stopping first to take the necessary photos of the room while it is in its pristine check-in condition. I would love to take a vacation, enjoy a meal at a restaurant, grab a coffee, go shopping, or do literally *anything* without feeling the need to document *every.single.thing*. After all, these are amazing content opportunities that I shouldn't neglect.

It might not seem like it, but I really do love doing this. I love to share content that inspires others or seeks to improve their lives, but at the same time I'm wondering if there is any opportunity for success in this industry with that kind of thinking any more. I honestly miss a simpler time when Instagram was just a photo-sharing app. We could just organically post photos of what we loved or felt inspired by, rather than having to carefully plan a post, ensure it fits perfectly into the grid, balance it with enough video content so that it gets considerable views, and tie it all up in a nice little bow with some story frames.

I wish that influencers would be more discerning with the work they chose, ensuring they *actually* like a product before endorsing it, or that it aligns with their brand rather than just selling ad space to the highest bidder. I long for the days when influencers were deemed "everyday tastemakers" and approachable creatives instead of untrustworthy, self-involved sellouts who make unreasonable demands as if they're pop stars.

I'm a Blogger at Heart

I've always considered myself to be a blogger first and an influencer second for so many reasons. For one, I own my blog and all of the content that I publish, whereas once something has been posted to Instagram, it is the property of that platform. I also believe that blog posts are a better value for a brand looking for authentic advertising content. Instagram is fleeting; a user scrolls past a photo and then moves on. Blog posts are permanent pieces of content that can be found in searches again and again.

The platform that hosts my blog is my ownership and responsibility, and I alone can determine if a post is deleted or not.

The Instagram app has experienced several outages over the past couple of years. Aside from realizing what a true addiction scrolling through this app is to so many (*Yikes! Go play outside!*), I watched influencers panic as they feared the loss of their entire business.

I've witnessed influencers scramble when Instagram has deleted their posts without reason or warning, because one of Instagram's bots incorrectly flagged their post as violating some internal policy. In turn, the brand they were working with nullified the contract and they lost thousands of dollars in income they were counting on. This is all because influencers have built their brands on a platform that they don't own.

Even if you don't buy in to the hype of social media, the truth is, there is a lot of money to be made marketing products on Instagram. Instagram is the platform of choice for most brands to advertise on and influencer marketing doesn't seem to be going anywhere anytime soon.

You might love some influencers and hate others but they're all playing the same game.

After all, to make a living, we're all just *chasing likes.*

ABOUT THE AUTHOR

Carlee Krtolica is the editor-in-chief of the highly acclaimed lifestyle blog, *Styled to Sparkle*, where she shares helpful advice on everything from interior design and DIY renovations to wine, travel, fashion, beauty, family, and more.

She has always naturally offered advice and shared what she loves with friends, family, and strangers. Carlee believes in making life more accessible for her audience especially through her love of the outdoors, global travel, home renovation and décor projects.

Throughout her influencer career she has collaborated with a number of well-known international brands such as IKEA, Wayfair, Bed Bath & Beyond, buybuy BABY, Cabela's, J.Crew, Hyatt, and Samsonite.

Carlee has a Bachelor of Commerce Degree majoring in Entrepreneurship, as well as her Wine & Spirits Education Trust Level 2 Certification. She currently works as a freelance interior designer and lifestyle blogger.

She lives in Canada with her husband, two daughters and dog named Hattie. Follow along on her social media channels @styledtosparkle.

Made in the USA
Monee, IL
22 January 2022